Faith Without Hostages

The Cross and Resurrection in Our Lives Today

———•———

HARRIET HARRIS

Published in Great Britain in 2002 by
Society for Promoting Christian Knowledge
Holy Trinity Church
Marylebone Road
London NW1 4DU

British Library Cataloguing-in-Publication Data
A catalogue record for this book is available from the British Library

ISBN 0-281-05479-7

10 9 8 7 6 5 4 3 2 1

Designed and typeset by Kenneth Burnley, Wirral, Cheshire.
Printed in Great Britain by Antony Rowe, Chippenham, Wiltshire.

Contents

Preface

Christ lived and taught a faith that held no one hostage. The reflections in this book celebrate this faith in the face of all the ways that religion can constrain and diminish us, make us afraid or ashamed, and leave us excluded or wanting to exclude others. Jesus lived and died fighting the forces that enslave us. He rose again free from those forces and from the resentments they cause.

This book is not a traditional Lent book, but takes us beyond the cross to the new life of Eastertide. It may be followed in these seasons, or it may be read at any time of the year for its various themes. The book invites you to read the biblical passages cited, and to reflect on them with the help of the comments and questions provided. This may be done on your own or with a group. I will say a bit here about the shape of the book, to help you decide how to use it.

The book begins with the disciples following Jesus as he turns towards Jerusalem, knowing that he is going to his death. The next few reflections consider what an enigmatic figure Jesus is, and how following him and drawing closer to God involves prayer, action and struggle, giving things up, taking risks and resisting evil. There are then three particular reflections, 'Reacting to exclusion', 'Christ and the Temple', and 'Incarnation and shame', on overcoming the evils of prejudice and oppression. 'Widows' through to 'On trial' consider the responses we make to God. With 'A Jesus we can believe in', the focus turns explicitly to Christ's suffering on the cross. Here Jesus is seen less as a passive victim than as a strong defender of good against evil. If you are following this book through Lent, you may wish to do the 'Meditations on the seven last words from the cross' throughout Holy Week, or particularly on Good Friday. I have tried to create a more contemplative feel around the meditations, following each one with a prayer rather than with questions.

A few final thoughts on using the book. You may like to note your own responses to the biblical passages before turning to the written reflections offered here. As for these written reflections, those other than the meditations on the words from the cross are divided in two to provide pause for thought. The two halves need not be read in one go, especially since some reflections are longer than others! If you find your thoughts running in quite different directions from those suggested by the questions, then do set the questions aside rather than let them constrict you. The book ends with reflections on Christ's resurrection and ascension. The conviction here, as at the start of the book, is that Christ lives, and that when we recognize his presence among us we can transform one another and the places where we live. I hope and pray that this book will play some small part in enabling such a transformation.

Oxford, May 2002

Acknowledgements

I am immensely grateful to Mark Harris, Jonathan Herapath, Brian Mountford, Helen O'Sullivan, Lydia Saunders, Lynn Trainor and Sian Williams for their comments on earlier versions of these reflections.

I would also like to thank Ruth McCurry at SPCK who commissioned and edited the collection, and the following copyright holders for permission to use the respective writings:

Kingsley Amis, 'New Approach Needed', copyright © Kingsley Amis, reprinted by kind permission of Jonathan Clowes Ltd, London, on behalf of the Literary Estate of Sir Kingsley Amis;

Janet Morley, 'Psalm of Grief', from *Human Rites: Worship Resources for an Age of Change*, compiled and edited by Hannah Ward and Jennifer Wild (London: Mowbray, 1995). Reprinted by kind permission of Continuum Books.

To the people of the
University Church of St Mary the Virgin, Oxford,
to Mark and to Benjamin

The glory and the shame

Luke 9.28–36

When Jesus leaves his own region of Galilee and turns his face towards Jerusalem, he is going to the place where he will die. This is the point where the event known as the Transfiguration occurs, when Jesus' appearance is transformed and for a short while he looks like a glorified or dazzling being. It is a pivotal moment. The disciples who are with Jesus on the mountain do not know what tragedy awaits them in Jerusalem. They do not know what struggles they will have to go through, nor what shame will come upon Jesus and themselves. As they are turning in the direction of Jerusalem, about to face the severest of trials, this sign on the mountain gives them a glimpse of Jesus' real identity. With hindsight they will come to understand that it is a sign of hope; a vision of Jesus' future glory.

Entering Lent is like beginning that journey to Jerusalem; and as with those who walked with Jesus, we do not know what awaits us. It is like going with Moses into the wilderness. When Moses led the Israelites out of Egypt, they had to keep reminding themselves that God had promised the Holy Land. Wandering in the desert, they felt lost and abandoned, much as the disciples must have felt when Jesus was arrested. Jesus himself felt abandoned too, by his friends and also by God.

On the mountain Jesus talks with Moses and Elijah. They were prophets who had both suffered to bring to Israel the liberty God intended. According to Jewish tradition, they had both been taken up into heaven. So they talk about the 'departure' Jesus is to accomplish at Jerusalem. This is a reference to Jesus' death, but the word for 'departure' is the word *exodus* – the same word used for Moses' flight from Egypt. Jesus is the Moses of the new covenant; of God's new pledge to save us. Moses led Israel through the desert to their freedom. Jesus leads not only Israel but all people into freedom.

When we go into Lent, we enter the wilderness. We take the path that leads to the desolation of Maundy Thursday when Jesus is betrayed, the horror and degradation of Good Friday when he is put to death, and the silence of Holy Saturday when we can do nothing but wait. Many Christians wonder why we should bother. If observing Lent means pulling up your spiritual socks, either by giving up things that please the body or by taking on extra worthy commitments, what virtue is there in trying to do this for only 40 days in a year? Shouldn't we always aim to live as we aspire to live in Lent? After all, every day is Lent, just as every day is Good Friday, and every day is Easter. I was once in a church with a friend who was offended that the crosses had been covered over for Lent as a sign of mourning. 'He did rise from the dead, you know', she said. Yes, but he also hung on the cross, and before that endured the struggle of facing what was coming his way. There is a time for weeping, a time for mourning and a time for keeping silent. There are other times for laughing, for dancing, and for speaking. Lent trains us for the wilderness, for the times when we are faced with loss, disappointment, or terror. It strips us of our own resources, and helps us learn to trust that God will bring us through the wilderness, probably in ways that we cannot ourselves foresee.

Turning towards Jerusalem, the disciples were soon to face a time when they would really have to doubt God's presence in Jesus, especially because the form of death that Jesus met was so terrible. Perhaps the most important point of the Transfiguration is that it puts Christ's terrible death in the context of glory.

Crucifixion is an abomination that has been passed over in silence. Crucifixions were carried out all around the Mediterranean world by the Greeks, Persians and Romans, but hardly anything is written about them because they were so hated and feared. They were a particular abomination for the Jews because of the law in Deuteronomy that casts out anyone who hangs upon a tree: 'When someone is convicted of a crime punishable by death and is executed, and you hang him on a tree, his corpse must not remain all night upon the tree; you shall bury him that same day, for anyone hung on a tree is under God's curse' (Deuteronomy 21.22–23).

Jesus' first followers had to face the shame of his execution in ways that we can barely imagine. We are so used to the idea that Jesus was crucified that we have become quite immune to it. We see crosses all around us, many of them decorous. We wear them as jewellery, and parade them as signs of both political and spiritual power, almost like military banners. But for the disciples the cross would have been far more shaming than the forms of state execution our civilization has since devised: more devoid of humanity than public killings by hanging or guillotine in front of jeering crowds; more undignified than being burnt from the inside out on an electric chair before a private audience. Because not only was there gloating, but there was the very basic humiliation of nakedness, there was the likelihood of abuse from the Roman soldiers, and there was the political shame of an occupying power displaying their might. And, in the case of Jesus, there was the added spiritual shame of the person in whom they had invested so much hope, dying like a criminal under Roman law, and as an outcast under Jewish law.

———— ·◆· ————

In the ancient world, as indeed in many cultures today, dying for one's people was an ideal, as these famous lines from Horace testify: 'dulce et decorum est pro patria mori', fitting and honourable it is to die for one's country. This is a sentiment we have come to distrust, especially after the First World War when young soldiers, many of whom had been eager to enlist, died ignoble, demeaning deaths.

But still today there are cultures where voluntary self-sacrifice for the sake of your people is considered honourable. Here is how a Japanese pilot in the Second World War wrote to his parents before a suicide mission: 'Please congratulate me. I have been given a splendid opportunity to die . . . I shall fall like a blossom from a radiant cherry tree . . . How I appreciate this chance to die like a man! . . . Thank you, my parents . . . I hope my present deed will in some small way repay what you have done for me.' He shares something in common with the more recent Muslim suicide bombers and hijackers, who have become folk heroes to hard-pressed Muslim communities around the world, their pictures paraded by schoolchildren carrying guns in the Middle East. They believe that their martyrdom makes them fit for immediate entry into paradise. Each of these types of martyr is regarded by their own people as noble, although to others they are dangerous and seem perverse.

What of Jesus' death? Could any of Jesus' contemporaries have seen glory in his crucifixion? This was unlikely. To the inhabitants of first-century Palestine, Jesus was not an ancient hero; he was a local Jewish craftsman only recently executed. A noble, honourable death is not the same as a criminal, base death. Jesus' execution did not ennoble him. It did not improve his image, but turned him into an easy target for people to mock and deride. It was not the kind of demise anyone would stage. It was not powerful in any conventional sense. It was bloody and sordid and demeaning. The idea of a crucified Messiah repulsed people. Contemporaries of the early Christians thought it a dark or even mad superstition.

We too steer clear of the sinister and insane nature of crucifixion. We find it distasteful at best that people in the Philippines re-enact Christ's death in a real-life way, actually flogging people and nailing them up on crosses. They seem to us to have gone too far, to have gone over the edge into a kind of madness. Perhaps being horrified by this behaviour is related to our distrust of Horace's sentiment; a sentiment made infamous by Wilfred Owen's graphic denunciation of it in a poem describing the effects of a gas attack:

> If you could hear at every jolt, the blood
> Come gargling from the froth-corrupted lungs,
> Obscene as cancer, bitter as the cud
> Of vile, incurable sores on innocent tongues, –
> My friend, you would not tell with such high zest
> To children ardent for some desperate glory
> The old Lie: Dulce et decorum est
> Pro patria mori.
> (Wilfred Owen, 'Dulce et Decorum Est', December 1917)

But the cross is a kind of madness, and so are the killing fields. Realizing this helps us to appreciate, as though for the first time, the shock and the power of the Transfiguration. The Transfiguration is astonishing because it turns this blood and gore, this humiliation and insanity, into Christ's glory. If we do not keep both the shame and the glory before our eyes, we can fall into two traps: first, of sitting too lightly to Jesus' crucifixion and treating it like an old, familiar story; and second, of being unprepared and vulnerable to defeat when suffering comes our own way.

Just before he went up the mountain, Jesus warned his disciples: 'If any want to become my followers, let them deny themselves and take up their cross daily and follow me.' And so we are to understand that somehow it is through suffering that we become like Christ. If at Lent we give up certain things that feed our bodies, we make ourselves all the more aware that our strength comes from God. When we receive ash on our foreheads on Ash Wednesday, we remind ourselves that we are but dust, and cannot live unless God breathes life into us.

Going into Lent is like the turn towards Jerusalem. At this juncture, the Transfiguration is presented as a gift to us. It is a sign of God's promise, given just as the worst of all things is about to happen. Perhaps we will lose sight of it, as the disciples did until after the Resurrection. Our reactions to signs of God's presence are like that: they ebb and flow. Moments of great poignancy are forgotten and then recalled again. That is how faith is: it does not ascend from one great revelation to the next, it moves through life's ups and downs, recalling some moments and then others. The Transfiguration, when we recall it, is a promise that gives us hope. The contrast between the dazzling moment on the mountain and the debased hours on the cross is the space where we live. It is the space that allows for unforeseen good to follow from unspeakable evils. The cross does not cancel out the glory. The glory does not mean there will be no cross.

———— •◆•————

For reflection

1 If Jesus had not been crucified, but had been given official honours for his service to the community, would the Christian faith have been different?

2 Is it important to you how Jesus died?

3 Robert Runcie used to say of the cross: 'To the Greeks foolishness, to the Jews a stumbling block, and to the English a perpetual source of embarrassment.' How do you cope with this difficult side to our faith?

4 Could there be an easier way, than the way of the cross, to get to the Promised Land, or to get to Easter?

5 What sort of encouragement does the story of Jesus' Transfiguration offer us?

2

We don't need another Messiah

John 10.22–39

Ten years ago the sportsman and TV personality David Icke was claiming to be the Son of God. When Icke was interviewed on the Wogan show, Terry Wogan asked him, 'Why you?', meaning, why would God pick you, or what makes you so special? 'People said the same thing about Jesus', Icke replied. 'Who the heck are you? You're the carpenter's son.' He had a point. Jesus was not that obvious a candidate. So how do you recognize the Son of God?

When the Jews ask Jesus to tell them plainly whether he is the Messiah, his answer fills them with murderous rage and they take up stones to hurl at him. It's not hard to see why. They are angry because Jesus said he was one with the Father. In the 1960s, John Lennon claimed that the Beatles were bigger than Jesus. The notoriety of this comment has outlived him. Jesus' claim to share his identity with God was more audacious and offensive than John Lennon's claim, and harder for his hearers to accept. There was nothing flippant in what Jesus was saying, and his words struck at people's religious convictions about the nature of God, and not just at their sense of propriety.

So Jesus' claims about himself upset the Jews. But the Jews must also have been incensed by his attitude towards them. Instead of answering them plainly, or even engaging them in debate, he tells them in effect that they are deaf and blind. Only his sheep have heard his voice and seen his works, and have understood. If you are not of Jesus' flock, you simply don't understand. Or conversely, if you don't understand, then you are not of his flock. (Jesus would not be enticed into religious apologetics.)

Not surprisingly, this frustrates and infuriates his inquisitors.

What do you do with someone who thinks you are deaf and blind? You cannot argue with him, because he believes you have no understanding. Jesus leaves his inquisitors with no mental ammunition, so they take up stones instead.

Could it have been that obvious that Jesus was the Messiah? Commentators on this passage from John's gospel tend to take the line that Jesus' works should have been enough for the Jews to understand. This is the logic of the narrative. The story is told in such a way that we blame the Jews for being dim-witted and hard of heart. But I wonder how well we would have fared had we lived in Jesus' day. Would we have recognized Jesus as the Christ whom we have come to embrace at 2,000 years' distance? I used to think that Jesus' contemporaries had an unfair advantage over us, in that they saw Jesus in the flesh, or at least saw the effects that he had on others. But now I think the opposite. We stand on the shoulders of generations of people who have had faith, and we are helped by them – the communion of saints down the ages whose understanding has shaped our own. If in my imagination I transport myself back to first-century Palestine, I worry for my salvation. I am not sure I would have seen what Jesus' followers were supposed to see. By the same token, I do not feel sure that if Jesus lived among us today, I would recognize him.

You either see it or you don't. That's what Jesus seems to be saying in John's gospel. This gospel was written for a persecuted and vulnerable community, which helps to explain its almost violent 'us and them' attitude. John's community had been driven out of the synagogue because they professed that Jesus was the Messiah. Having been expelled from the synagogue, they were most probably exposed to Roman persecution. The Romans tolerated Jews, but not Christians who were disclaimed by Jews. John's community will have had to make sense of their beleaguered state, and of why the Jews rejected their Messiah. So the tone of John's gospel is often quite cultish. It makes me think of our modern-day leaders of cults who regard themselves and their followers as uniquely elected to see the truth.

Of all those claiming to be messiahs today, the one with the biggest following is Sai Baba. Admirers from around the world flock to his ashram in India, and he purportedly has over 50 million devotees. Like Jesus, he is said to have created food to feed the masses, to have healed the sick on numerous occasions, and to have raised at least two people from the dead. He claims that Jesus was a minor avatar (an earthly manifestation of a deity), while he himself is the major avatar.

Sai Baba has received criticism, for sure, most notoriously for alleged sexual abuse of young men and boys. But, his devotees say, every great religious teacher has faced criticism. In their eyes, with every criticism levelled at Sai Baba he just becomes more triumphant. I suppose one could say, you either see it or you don't.

We know that Jesus courted controversy, and was accused of being a glutton and a wine-bibber, a law-breaker and blasphemer. He wasn't that obvious a candidate for messiah-status, and when he died the way he did, publicly shamed and cursed by Jewish law, deserted by, let's face it, the very small number of followers he had retained, his credibility was virtually zero. If we did not have the Christian tradition to inform and support us, a tradition that is now mainstream but was once wild and strange, would we recognize Christ? Do we really have the ears to hear and the eyes to see God's truth?

———— •◆• ————

The journalist Jon Ronson has recently followed up various self-proclaimed messiahs, and found them all utterly resistible. He finds them resistible because, he says, 'I was brought up by Jews who said that the Messiah will return not as a man but as a God . . . Perhaps if some huge powerful force arrives on Earth, surrounded by billowing smoke and dry ice and lasers . . . maybe then I will know the time has come.' However, Christians cannot have that kind of defence against false messiahs, because we already believe that God has come in the form of an ordinary human being. God did not come as a super-hero, but as someone born in humble circumstances, who lived as a mere carpenter in Galilee and died on a cross.

But a follower of Sai Baba asks, 'If God can incarnate once, why can't he incarnate as many times as he wants?' How can we hold that Jesus of Nazareth was God and yet dismiss all other would-be messiahs as impostors?

Well, because we do not need another messiah. What Jesus showed us was more than enough for us, and we have yet to take on board what he revealed.

Jesus showed us a Messiah who was very unsuccessful in the eyes of the world. He could attract a crowd, but he did not attract many devoted followers – just a handful really, and they abandoned him under pressure. He amassed no worldly goods, and did not store up arms as the freedom fighters did in his day, and as many cult leaders do in our own day. He was accused of many things, but he was not accused of manipulating or abusing people. He seems to have had a fairly light touch with his disciples, and wondered why they were so slow to understand him. At the same time, he never fully explained himself, and was reticent about his identity. Were he a twenty-first-century incarnation, he would probably not appear on television claiming to be the Son of God. He was called lord and master, but he washed his disciples' feet. He seemed neither to demand nor expect to be served. He regarded himself as a shepherd who looks after his flock, as one who goes out in search of a single lost sheep. And, the final twist, the shepherd turns out to be a lamb (Revelation 5.6–13) – one of the least powerful, least cunning, and least vain of creatures; an easy target, a sacrificial victim.

We do not need another messiah. We can find God in the humblest of human beings and in the rudest of stuff, in even the bread that we break. Jesus did not explain himself to us, and he did not explain God to us, but he showed us that God is with us and he showed us what God cares about. The world really has seen Christ, even if not fully recognizing him, because we now know to look for God in humble places: in the starving child, or the refugee, or the nursing mother, or the doting father, and even in bread and wine that we make with our own hands from stuff that grows from the ground, which is such basic food and drink for us.

If Christ had never come, it would seem a blasphemy to identify God with the crude stuff, and especially with the neglected people of this world. But Christ has come, and it no longer seems so strange to see God in such routine and mundane activities as preparing a meal, or in the eyes of those who are starving and diseased. Yet, most would-be messiahs behave as though this were in fact a blasphemy, and as though their worldly success in amassing wealth and followers should convince people of their divine status. We have to be open to God's presence anywhere and in anyone, but we are not looking for another incarnation, because Christ's body remains among us. Nor are we looking for a glitzy incarnation, because we now know this is not God's style.

For reflection

1   If Jesus were to walk on earth again as he did in first-century Palestine, what do you think he would be doing?
2   Do you think we would recognize him?
3   Do you think you would follow him?
4   Would he offend people?
5   In what ways is it true that Christ still lives on earth among us?

3

What would Jesus do?

Matthew 8.18–34

You may have noticed in recent years t-shirts, keyrings, necklaces and bracelets for sale bearing the letters WWJD. These letters stand for 'What Would Jesus Do?'. They are to remind you to ask yourself, in whatever situation, 'What would Jesus do if he were here now?' so that you can then go and do likewise. But Jesus is a man who sleeps on a boat through the fiercest of gales. When he is woken, instead of helping to bail out, as presumably you or I would, he speaks to the winds and the sea. Moreover, his mere presence brings scary men out of tombs and provokes the demons within them. How many of us could, let alone would, behave as these stories say that Jesus did?

The question 'What would Jesus do?' plays down just how odd and mysterious a person Jesus was. It is a helpful question in one sense because we need to concentrate on what we have in common with Jesus, and how we can imitate him. A central Christian belief is that Jesus was fully human: he became flesh, he dwelt among us, he ate and slept, he needed time alone, he wept, he got angry, he loved, he died. We can try to follow his example only if he was like us. It is crucial that he knew adversity and human frailty, otherwise what could we learn from him?

But in many ways, Jesus was not like us. When he calmed the storm, his disciples asked, 'What sort of man is this, that even the winds and the sea obey him?'

I have noticed from some recent novels that writers who are not believers sometimes do better than Christians at conveying the mysterious nature of Jesus. Perhaps they are less concerned to make Jesus like us, and so are freer to evoke the mystery of Jesus' union with God.

Jim Crace, a British author, wrote a book called *Quarantine* about people who went into the wilderness to fast, and who happened to be sharing the desert with Jesus. These people were fascinated by Jesus. They tried to tempt him out of his cave to break his quarantine, but they never managed to meet or speak to him. Crace describes Jesus at the end of his fast as someone who is 'full of God at last'. Earlier in the book he hints at what it might mean to be full of God, and how one could get to that state. He writes,

> [Jesus] did not need to move his lips to pray. He'd reached the stage where every breath was prayer, where all the steps and sounds he made were verses for God, where everything was touched with holiness: a heel of bread, the soundless corners of the house when he woke up, the cobwebbed shadows on the clay-white walls, the motes of sawdust hanging in the window light, the patterns on his fingertips. God in everything and everything in God. (p. 74)

The American novelist Norman Mailer, a prodigal son if ever there was one, surprised the literary world in the late 1990s by writing a life of Jesus from Jesus' own perspective. He called it *The Gospel According to the Son*. This is a highly audacious thing to do, but Mailer pulls it off pretty well. When he retells the story from the gospels that we are now considering, this is what he has Jesus say on confronting the Gadarene demoniac:

> I knew he was filled with devils – so many that they might be too much for me. Yet the hand of the Lord was on my back and urging me forward. 'The unclean spirits who devoured King Herod are now in you,' I said. 'Flee from Legion. Flee.' And I growled like a beast, which is what the Essenes do to enforce a commandment they receive from the Lord. (p. 94)

My sense is that Christian accounts of Jesus' life present us with a more normal Jesus than do either Crace or Mailer. They can deliver a stronger call to action by showing us a Jesus who is more like us. I am thinking especially of Gerd Theissen's *The Shadow of the Galilean*. This is a hard-hitting book. It tells the Gospel indirectly from the perspective of a man, Andreas, who has heard of Jesus' subversive reputation for mixing with outcasts and championing the causes of the poor.

Andreas travels around Palestine in Jesus' shadow, stumbling across communities that have been completely turned around by Jesus' actions. On the way to Bethsaida he meets a toll-collector called Kostabar who is having some trouble with beggars and children. Kostabar has taken Levi's job after Levi left to follow Jesus. 'They used to be happy if you gave them bread', Kostabar explains. 'But since people like Jesus and Levi have raised their hopes they've become more importunate. They're waiting for the great turning point, the kingdom of God. Then they'll sit at richly decked tables with Jesus, the halt and the lame, the wheezers and the derelicts . . . Meanwhile they live with these fantastic hopes, with demands which no village, no town, no one can fulfil. With demands which belong in another world, not in our land.' As Andreas sets off again on his way he is stopped by some children playing at toll-collectors. 'This is the beginning of the kingdom of God', they say. 'We rule in this kingdom . . . The kingdom of God is ours.' 'And what duty must I pay?' Andreas asks. 'Give us something to eat', they say. 'Is that all?' he asks. 'There is no kingdom you can enter so easily. All you must do is give away what you possess. Then you belong to it.' So Andreas learns about the radical Jesus who disturbs us with his incredibly simple, incredibly hard demands.

But he does not learn about Jesus' mysterious presence.

Theissen is a biblical scholar trying to recover what one can of the historical Jesus of Nazareth. The trend in his field of work, historical Jesus research, is to make Jesus appear as ordinarily human as possible. As Christians, we are often concerned to make Jesus look like a normal bloke with radical ideas. Think of the Church of England poster campaigns featuring the laughing Jesus, or Jesus as Che Guevara. We fight shy of presenting Jesus as prayerful, as having mystical power, as holy.

———— • ◆ • ————

One of the most interesting scenes in Mailer's book is a conversation between Jesus and Judas, where the tension is played out between devoting oneself to radical action in the world and withdrawing into contemplation. Judas says he follows Jesus because, 'in the course of saying all that you say, the poor will take courage to feel more equal to the rich'. But he does not believe in the kingdom of heaven, nor that Jesus 'will ever bring us all to salvation'. Jesus admires Judas' honesty and welcomes his hard work, which he thinks will 'help to bring us all to salvation'. He asks Judas, 'If I ceased to labour – by even a jot or a tittle – for the needs of the poor, would you see less value in me?' Judas replies, 'I would turn against you. A man who is ready to walk away from the poor by a little is soon ready to depart from them by a lot.'

So Jesus reflects that if all of his disciples had beliefs as powerful as Judas, he could be stronger and accomplish so much more. Yet he also senses that he will have trouble with Judas because Judas 'had none of the accommodation that my Father had given to my heart to make me ready for those trials that could come upon us unforeseen' (pp. 136–9). Judas only knew the social Gospel. He had not come to know God.

Mailer has a fundamental insight here. If Judas had come to know God like Jesus did, he could have withstood trials. The story of the calming of the sea makes a similar point. Jesus could sleep through the storm, because of his great trust in God. The disciples did not have so much trust in God, and had not yet learned who Jesus was. Therefore they were awake and fretful. When Jesus calms the storm, Mailer has him say: 'In the presence of my great joy on this night – and I was feeling great joy at having come so close to my Father – their hearts would harden. For they could not share my wonder' (pp. 118–19).

The story of the calming of the sea is about being followers of Jesus. If we look at the preceding verses, and bear in mind that the verb 'to follow' actually became a technical term in the New Testament for becoming a disciple of Jesus, the story becomes all the more striking:

When Jesus saw a crowd around him, he gave orders to cross to the other side. A scribe approached and said to him, 'Teacher, I will follow you wherever you go.' Jesus answered him, 'Foxes have dens and birds of the sky have nests, but the Son of Man has nowhere to rest his head.' Another of (his) disciples said to him, 'Lord, let me go first and bury my father.' But Jesus answered him, 'Follow me, and let the dead bury their dead.' He got into a boat and his disciples followed him. (Matthew 8.18–23)

The boat contains the people who followed Jesus. They did so having heard his demanding and hard-hitting teachings. No matter how much we try to do as Jesus would do, who among us would leave the dead to bury their dead? Indeed, how many among us reckon that doing as Jesus would do means forgoing the security of house and home? Jesus had said he had nowhere to lay his head, but his trust in God meant that he could lay his head anywhere, even in a small boat tossed about on stormy waters. He was at peace in any situation. Those who follow him (and in traditional interpretations, the boat in this story is thought to signify the Church) are encouraged to share Jesus' peacefulness even in the most precarious situations, and to trust in Jesus' power.

Judas saw that following Jesus means practising a radical Gospel of love, but did he see that it also means learning to trust God if we are to do God's work? Norman Mailer puts it in terms of having that accommodation of heart that God gives us to face unforeseen trials. It strikes me that writers who are not themselves Christians have been putting this very well. Jim Crace in *Quarantine* hits the nail on the head. He shows Jesus to be someone constantly in prayer, and he shows that this is hard work. It involves going into the wilderness where your prayers could actually be swallowed up by the darkness, and cease to be of comfort, so that you have to persevere through the stretches where you draw no solace from prayer. Crace manages to convey that because Jesus constantly opened himself up to God, he drew people to him. In doing so drew them to God.

———•◆•———

For reflection

1 Is it ever justifiable to spend time alone with God when you could be spending it helping others? Are you someone who shuts yourself away to pray?

2 Why are we as Christians often shy of presenting Jesus as a wonder-worker and mystic?

3 Would Jesus today be involved in social action? What kind of action would he undertake?

4 How would his involvement differ from that of someone like Judas?

5 How can we today be people who are like Jesus?

4

Extravagance and waste

Philippians 3.4b–14

For his sake I have suffered the loss of all things, and I regard them as rubbish, in order that I may gain Christ. (Philippians 3.8b)

This is a sanitized translation of Paul's infamous reference to human excrement. I contrasted various Bible translations to see which would give the word *skubala* its proper filthy meaning. The most recent versions say 'rubbish' or 'garbage', which shows how refined we've become! The most general meaning of the term is 'refuse', and given that both household and human waste would have ended up on the same refuse heap, our modern, bowdlerized translations are not technically wrong. But the Authorized Version and most nineteenth-century translations were less coy, using the word 'dung'. I suppose an equivalent today (not a literal equivalent, but an equivalent in sentiment) would be 'bullshit', which comes fairly close to Paul's meaning. He is saying that all the past things of his life, things we would naturally regard as respectable and worth striving for, are bullshit, meaningless, and he used an expletive to shock and offend his audience's sense of respectability.

He is still offending his audiences today. If we weren't offended we might write 'shit' in our Bibles instead of 'rubbish'. But we shy away from both the earthiness and the vehemence of Paul's message. Is this partly because we still identify with the old Paul? The old Paul was proud of being good at what he did. This we can understand. We hope to be good at what we do. We feel secure and gratified when we achieve certain things, and insecure and discontent when we think we fail. But Paul says it's all a load of crap. The new Paul wants to share Christ's sufferings and become like him in his death, although he knows this will bring him no earthly security and very little respect. No doubt people thought he was wasting his life, 'throwing it all away', which is a charge anyone faces who gives up things for God.

Are we, in our particular churches and communities, people of relatively high- and good-standing in society? If so, how do we need to hear Paul? We know from Paul's life and teaching that it wasn't because he had forsaken his past credentials that he gained Christ. He gained Christ because Christ came and claimed him. We know the dramatic story of Paul's vision on the Damascus road. It is because Christ came to Paul that Paul took this U-turn in life, and from his new perspective came to see his past as worthless.

Meanwhile, Paul says, we still have to work hard. I wonder how you find Paul's talk of 'pressing on toward the goal'? I respond quite negatively to it because it can seem like salvation by works. I have been in contexts where Christians are effectively taught to strive to please God: to pray harder, read your Bible for longer, give more of your time to witnessing to Christ. A lot of churches became this way in the Thatcher years, and have not yet shaken off the mentality. I once did a discipleship course and was given a time-sheet to fill in, indicating how I spent each 15 minutes of the subsequent six weeks. Of course, such churches are following the practices of secular institutions that try to maximize productivity. But churches ought to know better. If we feel we have to strive in our relationship with God, it is very difficult to find peace in God because we can always think that we haven't done enough. The flip-side to striving is feeling that God is displeased with us, and that we have somehow to earn God's favour.

It is a matter of getting things the right way round. Paul says, 'I want to know Christ . . . because Christ Jesus has made me his own.' Paul's efforts are a response to what Christ has already done. Christ has claimed Paul, and this is why Paul reacts with such enthusiasm, and why he sheds his old identity so completely. Christ re-created him on the road to Damascus. He sowed new seeds in Paul that bore new fruit.

———— •◆• ————

On his way to Jerusalem, Jesus stops over in Bethany at the house of Lazarus, Mary and Martha (John 12.1–8). Mary anoints Jesus' feet with expensive perfume and wipes them with her hair. In many ways, it is a lovely thing that Mary does; a moment of intimacy sand-wiched between two sinister episodes in Jesus' journey. Just before he had reached Bethany the chief priests and Pharisees had given orders for Jesus' arrest. Then straight after Mary anoints Jesus' feet, Judas begins to oppose him, saying 'Why was this perfume not sold for three hundred denarii and the money given to the poor?' So Mary's exuberant hospitality is a piece of sweetness in an otherwise bitter time. Jesus enjoys it while he can, but sees in it a sign of his death. 'Leave her alone,' he says to Judas. 'She bought [the perfume] so that she might keep it for the day of my burial. You always have the poor with you, but you do not always have me.'

But others are irritated by Mary, and I think I would have been too. Judas speaks for many when, whatever his underlying intentions, he says the money would have been better spent on the poor. No doubt many of us feel this way when we think about the riches in the great cathedrals around the world, and in any wealthy Christian commu-nity. Should churches have wealth that is not directed to the poor? Does having extravagantly beautiful things in church suggest that we have our priorities wrong? Or does it suggest that we have them right?

Mary's use of wealth is just one gripe against her. Another is that Mary sits at Jesus' feet while her sister Martha runs around provid-ing food, and it doesn't seem fair. Okay, Mary has a better sense than Martha of when to be still and to listen. Perhaps Martha is an incurable fuss-pot. But when Mary wipes Jesus' feet with her hair, she seems a bit of a floozie. If I am harsh on Mary, it is because of a sympathy for Martha and a dislike of exhibitionism. But my criti-cisms, I realize, are condemned by Jesus' attitude.

Jesus is excessive in his defence of Mary. He imparts to her an intention she may never have had. He says that the reason she bought the perfume was to keep it for the day of his burial. She prob-ably had no such thoughts. Hers was an act of personal devotion to Jesus, but Jesus judges her more generously and more extravagantly than that. This is how he makes people new – by defending us beyond what we deserve, and claiming us when we are not worthy.

Victor Hugo's novel *Les Misérables* tells of a person's life turned around by extravagantly kind judgement. Jean Valjean is caught stealing silver cutlery from a bishop, but the bishop tells the police that he has given them to Jean as a gift. As if this weren't enough, he even gives Jean some matching candlesticks. When the police are gone, the bishop tells Jean, 'You no longer belong to evil but to good. I have bought your soul.' Valjean starts to become a new man. His turn-around does not happen at once. At first he is angry. But he changes and devotes his life to saving others from evil. He takes a new name, calling himself Monsieur Madeleine. The name is a version of Magdalene, a reference to Mary Magdalene whose life was utterly transformed by meeting Jesus. According to one tradition, Mary Magdalene was the sister of Martha and the woman who anointed Jesus' feet with perfume. This tradition is no longer officially accepted by the Church, but the insight remains that both Mary Magdalene and Mary the sister of Martha and Lazarus were made new by Jesus' generous judgement of them.

Yes, Mary's perfume was extravagant and the 'waste' might offend us, as might the waste of people like Paul who turn their backs on their past achievements. But these mirror God's perpetual extravagance. Creation is extravagant, with so much abundance and so much going to waste. Our salvation is extravagant, bought with such a costly price, and with little guarantee that people will respond. And God's judgement of us abounds with generosity, holding us to be better than we really are. It is this extravagance, lavished on Paul who had been killing Christians for goodness' sake, that turns our lives around. And the irony is this, that when we see God's extravagance, we have to reassess our values: all that we would more naturally hold dear starts to look worthless in Christ.

———— •◆• ————

For reflection

1 In what sense are our family background, our education, our possessions and our qualifications 'rubbish'?
2 Do we need to change how we spend our money, how we acquire our money, the people we wish to impress, the things we aim to do well?
3 What do you think about having extravagantly beautiful things in church? Do they suggest that we have our priorities right, or wrong?
4 Do you ever feel that you need to earn God's favour? If so, how does this affect the way you pray, the way you spend your time, the way you are with family or friends?
5 What did Mary get right when she anointed Jesus' feet? In what ways might we imitate her?

Blood and barriers

Luke 8.41–56

'Only the periodic presence of women rescues the Bible from battle fatigue and worse,' says the sassy (though now drug-fixated) American writer Elizabeth Wurtzel in her book *Bitch*. 'Without women entering for the occasional intrigue, it would all be men doing their manly things – men sojourning and men wandering and men battling.' Without women, she wonders, 'who would supply the glamour? the suspense? the mystery? – women are the whole reason that the book is the all-time best-seller.'

Wurtzel is Jewish and is interested in the sexy seductresses of the Hebrew Bible. She is particularly impressed by Delilah, whose intimacy with Samson ultimately cost him his power. Wurtzel notes that all intimacy is threatening and potentially emasculating. This is so even when women aren't glamorous. Luke tells a story of an impoverished woman with unstoppable menstrual bleeding. She is vile in the eyes of her culture, and is cast out of community life because she is ritually impure. She is not the kind of woman you would see on the front of a glossy best-seller. Yet, like Delilah, she empties a man of his power. She touches the hem of Jesus' cloak, and he feels the power leave him.

I read an account of this passage which simply said that Jesus stopped on his way to Jairus' daughter in order to heal an old woman with an issue of blood. This does our woman no justice at all. Jesus stopped because he felt the power had left him. The initiative was hers. It was her resolution to cross borders of legitimate behaviour by placing herself in a dense crowd. The crowd's pressure was so menacing that it threatened to choke Jesus. People must have been pushing up against her as well. In their view, coming into contact with a bleeding woman would contaminate them. So the menacing crowd would not have looked kindly on this particular woman, whose mere presence threatened to taint them with her impurity. But she was not deterred. She presumed to touch Jesus – a man to whom even a synagogue ruler had bowed – and the power left him.

When a woman takes power from a man, she is frequently regarded as working some kind of feminine magic because, being physically weaker, she cannot overcome him by brute force. Transport this woman to sixteenth-century England, and we could imagine her being mistaken for some kind of witch: bloody and vile, and with powers to enfeeble the men she touches. She certainly wasn't sexy, but she was more gutsy than Delilah, who waited for Samson to fall asleep before calling in a man to cut his hair. This woman defied the socio-religious norms of her day that would have held her very much at arm's length. And so doing, she won for herself a blessing from God.

God does not berate us for having the audacity to resist practices and traditions that hurt us. Jesus seemed impressed by the woman who touched his cloak. He could have had her reprimanded. The law held her to be defiled until she had served seven days' quarantine ending in a sacrifice performed by a priest. He could have requested his own ritual purification, having been touched by her unclean hand. But he responded to her touch with intimacy. He was disarming but not disempowering. He called her 'daughter'. This was what finally made her whole. The physical healing was merely the outward sign – a sacrament, if you like. It was a physical sign of a deeper reality. The full healing of this woman came not when the bleeding stopped, but when Jesus called her out of her isolation, asked her to identify herself, and instituted her back into society by embracing her as a member of the family of God.

———— ◆ ————

Jesus finally made it to Jairus' house only to be told that the girl had already died. What would we have thought when Jesus insisted that she was sleeping? The mourners knew she was dead, and they laughed at Jesus. He spoke falsely by the standards of this world. He was one who, as was said by the prophet Isaiah, did not judge by what his eyes saw or decide by what his ears heard (Isaiah 11.3). And yet, Jesus was right. There was a sense in which the girl was alive and merely sleeping, and this was what he demonstrated by restoring her spirit to her.

We could suggest a naturalistic reading of the events: Jairus' daughter was in fact only unconscious, and Jesus simply restored her to full health. But this would distort the narrative and miss the point of the story. She was truly dead. Luke was careful to convey that. The thing to do here, I think, is neither to explain away the miracle, nor to be transfixed by it. I have read a number of student essays recently on the challenges of modern secularism, which argue that the way for religion to face secularist challenges is to become more scientific and less mysterious. I find this rather dated – a bit 1970s. And while 1970s style is fashionable at the moment in clothes and hair and kitchen design, it is not the fashion in religion. One of the most interesting and exciting trends in religion today is a desecularizing of nature, and a re-mystifying of God's relationship to the world. This trend is coming not only from traditional, sacramental churches which have down the centuries celebrated God's presence in mundane, physical, everyday things – most notably in the bread and wine of the communion meal – it is also coming from grass-roots movements which are not very churched, and which like to use modern media, but which want to tap the wisdom of ancient trad-itions. Let me try and describe a worship session as might be conducted within such a movement.

Imagine a church, or a community hall, or a room in a pub, with a music system and other technical equipment. There are candles, some icons, and something like dry ice, which turns out to be incense. You will also need to imagine a wall space large enough to project slides on to, and another place to show a home-made video. The ceiling might do. There is an installation near the door. And the slides, video and installation are following through a theme: God of the city, or the planetary mass, or faith in the poor. There are no pews or seats. People are standing or sitting on the floor, listening to ambient music – rave is no longer the thing, and choruses and plastic chairs are way out of date. Different people speak from various points in the room. The many activities and foci coincide, each inviting our attention. You can switch quickly from one thing to the next, like a person with a remote control flicking through the channels on a television set, or you can cruise like someone surfing the net, or you can become contemplative and fix on one thing as a focus for meditation. There is no centre to the worship, and no clear leader. This is decentred, alternative worship, aiming to be fully egalitarian and inclusive.

Then comes the Eucharist, and as if from nowhere there is a priest in our midst, in full vestments. All other activity is stopped and an altar is suddenly established as the focus. The eucharistic prayer is said with all the ritual and ceremonial that can be mustered (from whichever traditions people know or like), and the worshippers form lines to receive the bread and the wine: the body and the blood of Christ. It's a high mass in a low setting. What is it that these non-institutional, non-hierarchical Christians are saying about the sacraments, that they wish to have a priest and ceremonial to celebrate them? What is it that these non-traditional Christians are seeking in the old spiritual traditions?

It is, I think, a desire to respond to the sense of God's presence and power in the world. They have tired of a fully secularized world, in which nature is just nature to be fully comprehended by reason and science. They have tired of forms of religion that reflect such a secularized outlook; that suppose people must believe with their minds before they consent with their hearts; that give the pulpit primary place in a church building (and the preacher the primary voice); and that think that the way to make the sacraments accessible is to surround them with words of explanation. Instead, they want awe and mystery, and an undomesticated, non-rational God. It is not signs and wonders that they are looking for, because they have been there and done that. Many such worshippers have come out of charismatic churches where dramatic happenings are two a penny, and seem nothing more than a bit of divine intervention in an otherwise rationalized universe. Rather, they want an ongoing, all-pervasive sense of God's amazing presence in the mundane. In the midst of the hustle and bustle, the fractious-making hyper-activity of our technological culture, there is God. And there is God in the choking crowds in the narrow streets of first-century Jerusalem.

And what is God doing? Mysterious and powerful things, yes. But the way to respond to these is not to try explaining the mechanism by which they work, nor to regard them as some kind of divine magic, as though an impersonal power had passed from Jesus' cloak through the bleeding woman's fingertips to her womb. Jesus always discouraged that sort of attitude, which is perhaps why he ordered Jairus and his wife to tell no one about the reviving of their daughter, because it would encourage the crowds in their clamour to see miracles. The danger of focusing on the miraculous powers is that we might forget the prophetic truth to which they point. All of Jesus' miracles were demonstrations that God's kingdom is breaking through the powers that currently hold the world in its grip. These are the powers of death and of all that leads to death, including the seductive forces of superstition, suspicion and fear. Such forces cause us to erect barriers between one another, to neglect, and even to kill one another. So what is God doing in our midst? God is breaking down barriers, embracing outcasts, restoring people to community, restoring people to life.

————•◆•————

For reflection

1 The bleeding woman was an affront to her society. Who is an affront to our society today?

2 What barriers need breaking down between ourselves and others? How might we go about doing this?

3 How can the woman with a haemorrhage be a role model for us?

4 How do you think God's power works in the world? Can we be part of it? How is it communicated through worship, prayer, social action?

5 Do you believe there is more to the world than science can uncover? If so, what sort of experiences do you have for saying so?

6

Suffering and dread

Job 13.13—14.6

Virginia Woolf wrote an entry in her journal: 'I read the Book of Job today. God does not come out well in it.' Who could disagree with her? We don't see much of God's compassion in the Book of Job. Rather, we see a God who is apparently unmoved by Job's plight, and who seems to regard Job's family, labourers and animals as dispensable. Then like some cosmic bully, he (it is often said that the God of the Book of Job is a macho God) deflates Job by reminding him of his own divine power and might: 'Then the LORD answered Job out of the whirlwind: "Who is this that darkens counsel by words without knowledge? Gird up your loins like a man, I will question you, and you shall declare to me. Where were you when I laid the foundation of the earth?"' (Job 38.1–4a).

For all the Lord's bravado, it is Job who most impresses us in this book. Insofar as God's character is revealed here at all, it is best done so through Job's insistence that God is a God who must vindicate him. Chapter 13 of the book is a turning point, when Job for the first time demands an audience with God. He has lost his children, his livelihood, his home and his health. His friends, whom we have come to call 'Job's comforters', tell him that God is punishing him and that he must have done something wrong. So Job not only suffers extreme loss, pain and anguish, but also has to labour under the misguided view of his friends that his suffering is somehow deserved. They try to persuade him that his plight is reasonable and just. So Job has no one besides himself who recognizes the injustice of the situation and names it for what it is.

Often we need friends to help us get a right perspective on our situation. Friends can hold up mirrors for us in which we see ourselves more clearly. But if the mirrors are not straight, they create grotesque reflections of reality like you see in a fairground hall of mirrors. And then we have to turn the distorted mirrors to the wall, and stand alone before God.

This is what Job does. He has to silence his friends. He can hear no more of the twisted half-truths they are presenting to him. 'Let me have silence and I will speak,' he cries. And the person he wants to speak with is God. His friends' irrelevant clatter has actually become harmful. Whenever people rationalize injustice, their words do damage. They take you into a twilight zone where your sense of what is good and true is jeopardized by clever and seductive arguments – like coming too much under the influence of insidious propaganda.

The lie that Job's comforters told was an age-old lie that still has power over us today. This is the lie that all suffering is punishment for sin. The Book of Job was written to correct this misjudgement, but despite the great age of this book, people the world over still find the theory enticing. The suspicion is never far away that gays got what they deserved when AIDS came along. People want to see BSE and the spread of foot and mouth disease as come-uppance for immoral farming practices. (The animals are presumably innocent pawns in this game of consequences.) The suggestion lingers in the air that disabilities can be 'explained' as the result of past misdeeds, either the sins of our ancestors (in a Judaeo-Christian context), or, if you believe in reincarnation, the bad karma of our own past lives. Glenn Hoddle had to step down as England's football manager for expressing his belief that disabled people must have done some wrong in a previous life. And yet it emerged that many others share his views. This is not only because more and more people from a broadly Christian culture are interested in the Indian religions; it is also because there is something very enticing about being able to explain suffering. If we could understand why people suffer, we could perhaps control the forces that ravage us rather than be at their mercy. The deception that suffering is punishment seems hard for us to live without.

The inverse to this lie also has some grip on us: the idea that success is a sign of God's blessing. Norman Mailer, in an interview with *The Scotsman* (Summer, 2000), said 'there are black tribes in Africa that believe that if you're successful it is because God . . . has rewarded you . . . So successful people are immensely admired. And', he goes on to say, 'that is true here and now. There is a feeling of "Donald Trump is closer to God than I am".' This is also the message of Kingsway International Christian Centre in east London, which is currently the fastest growing church in Britain. This is at root a Nigerian Pentecostal Church. It teaches that success comes through living righteously and praying in power, and that unanswered prayers are the result of doing something wrong. Currently this church has over 6,000 members.

This way of thinking is attractive because we want to be able to explain things. We would like to make our good or bad fortune a simple matter of how well or badly we behave. It is the adult version of the story we tell children: that if they are good, Father Christmas will bring them what they want, and if they are bad they should expect to be disappointed. If suffering is punishment, then our fate is in our hands. If we don't like it, at least we can say we deserved it.

Such thinking is intensely damaging. Recently, someone I know from a church not dissimilar to Kingsway International had a stroke. He is only in his thirties, and has a wife and two small children. Now he is severely paralysed and having to learn how to talk again. Members of that church have in hushed tones been trying to work out just what it is that he has done wrong. This turns him and his family into pariahs just at the point where they need most support. Moreover, it rationalizes a suffering that they can experience only as irrational. If no one will sit with them in their bewilderment, then like Job, they will have to shut out the voices of their 'comforters' and stand alone before God, requesting an audience.

———— ◆ ————

It takes courage to know what Job knew, that he was not to blame for his troubles. What most impresses me about Job is not just that he knows he is righteous enough to demand a hearing from God, but that he sets down conditions for God's demeanour towards him. God is infinitely mightier than Job and could easily overwhelm him. So Job asks that God play by the rules of court: 'Behold I have prepared my case, he says; I know that I shall be vindicated . . . Only grant two things to me . . . withdraw your hand far from me, and let not dread of you terrify me.' Job is saying to God: stop impeding me, and don't intimidate me. Instead of letting a natural sense of dread deter him, Job asks God to remove it.

This is very significant, because we could interpret feelings of dread as an indication that we should back off: that we have trodden too close and have attempted to see things we should not see, just as Moses was not permitted to see the face of God (Exodus 33.18–23). I was recently participating in a consultation on genetic modification. There, one Christian philosopher argued against genetically modifying food on the grounds that we feel a kind of holy dread about tampering with nature to this degree. He said we should respect the dread as a godly fear, a sign not to meddle with God's creation in this way.

There are many good reasons for being extremely cautious about genetic modification (most of them to do with safety), but I suggest that holy dread is not one of them. People have felt holy dread about all sorts of things: rail travel, organ transplants, inter-racial marriages, women priests, drinking alcohol; the list goes on. And they have used this dread to erect sacred walls that we are not supposed to transgress. Often what we need to do is confront what lurks behind the dread, and say, 'Cut out the scare-mongering, and let's get a proper look at you.'

Job mentions his dread of God in the same context as his search for salvation. For this reason, I relate his concept of dread to Paul's talk about working out your salvation in fear and trembling (Philippians 2.12). It makes more sense to me to understand holy dread not as a sign to stop what you are doing, but as a sign that what you are doing is very significant. In his book *The Way of the Heart,* Henri Nouwen tells a story about a frail old man who had been roughly treated by demons and pulled to the floor by the devil. When he cried out, 'Jesus, save me', the devil fled away and the old man began to weep. Jesus asked him why he was weeping, and he said, 'Because the devils have dared to seize a man and treat him like this.' Nouwen's comment is that 'only in the context of the great encounter with Jesus Christ himself can real authentic struggle take place . . . it is precisely in the midst of this struggle that our Lord comes to us and says, as he said to the old man in the story: "As soon as you turned to me again, you see I was beside you."' The fear and trembling are signs that the encounter is authentic and significant.

We experience dread when we go with God to the places where

our own fears need conquering, where prejudices need confronting, and where worldly principalities and powers – I mean the injustices in this world – need to be overcome. Job confronted a stronghold. He confronted a system of religion that still has some power over us, and which says that our suffering is our just desert. In confronting that lie, not only is Job vindicated, but to some extent so is God. It is true that God does not come out very well in the Book of Job. If we know about God's love and compassion, it is not from reading this story. But what the Book of Job achieves, for those with ears to hear, is the demolition of that hideous belief that our suffering is God's punishment. And when that belief is brought down, God's reputation is redeemed to some extent. Sometimes we need to do work that makes us tremble in order to let God's truth emerge.

––––––•◆•––––––

For reflection

1   What makes you fear and tremble? Where is God in that struggle?
2   Have you ever had to struggle against prevailing opinion in order to vindicate yourself, or to vindicate God?
3   How have you or others you know experienced God in suffering: as absent, silent, combative, supportive, compassionate, or in some other way?
4   How can we best support others in their suffering?
5   Might feelings of holy dread sometimes indicate that we should stop what we are doing?

7

Cain and envy

Genesis 4.1–16

Having always felt sorry for Cain, I have come to see his story in relation to that of John the Baptist. Both Cain and John live with the discomforting awareness that their relatives, Cain's brother Abel, and John's cousin Jesus, are more favoured than them in God's sight. But their reactions could not have been more different. John seems unbelievably selfless and generous-spirited. Jesus 'must increase, but I must decrease', he says, seemingly happy to stand aside, to put himself out of the picture (John 3.30). Cain, on the other hand, is seized with envy, and he lets this envy eat away at him to the point where he kills his own brother. He becomes angry when God accepts Abel's offering but not his own. Hot resentment boils up in him and, we are told, his countenance falls. We can almost picture him: his face clouding over, eyes cast to the ground, shoulders hunched. We even have a colour for his particular ailment: green, the colour of envy, the colour of bile.

And why wouldn't Cain feel this way? His offering is spurned and God has shown favouritism to his brother. It seems deeply unfair. Writers have sought diligently for a reason why God might have favoured Abel over Cain. Of course, God can do whatsoever God pleases, and does not need to provide reasons, but is God then simply capricious?

To shift the blame away from God, some commentators have suggested that the two brothers were already on bad terms. Perhaps Cain had always been jealous of Abel, feeling displaced when the younger sibling came along. Perhaps God took against Cain because Cain was already a nasty piece of work, and murdering his brother was the outworking of a deeply flawed character. It is also possible that Cain's offering was second-rate and stingy. But the story as it comes to us in Genesis (possibly with clues that we do not know how to decipher) presents Cain as someone who is disfavoured for no apparent reason.

While this leaves us feeling morally uneasy about God, it is in fact one of the story's great strengths, because it helps us to identify with Cain. If Cain were described as a villain from the outset, we could hold him at arm's length and say that we are not at all like him. But since he comes to us as a hurt and wronged brother, he gets us on his side. We feel his hurt and indignation. We then have to decide how far we will go down the road he chooses to tread.

God warns Cain not to let sin devour him. 'Sin is lurking at the door, hungry to get you,' he says, 'but you must master it.' Envy is sometimes said to be morally neutral: not a sin in itself but an appreciation of loss, which can become either constructive or destructive. But traditionally it is regarded as one of the seven deadly sins, because of its power to ensnare us and to engender other sins. It can cultivate meanness, deceit and hatred, and can drive us towards death. But despite God's warning, Cain lets envy get the better of him, and envy is a murderous thing. He kills his brother, then lies about it, and at no point does he show any remorse. He feels sorry for himself, not because he regrets the murder, but because he thinks his punishment is too much to bear. (He fears that he will become a fugitive and prey to anyone who wants to kill him. He has not realized that God will protect him.) To avoid this descent into sin, what might Cain have done instead, when his offering was rejected?

Should he have accepted God's disfavour lying down? Was he wrong to feel angry? But what self-respecting person would not fight back? Imagine that this is a matter of civil rights. For all we know, Cain was a victim of discrimination, held in disregard for no apparent reason. Should we not do something about that kind of discrimination, rather than letting it go unchallenged? A leading scholar of the Book of Genesis, Claus Westermann, suggests from Cain's story that there is a positive element in envy, in that it enables you to react when you are rejected. After all, there is no virtue in being a doormat. It can be a moral response to feel sickened when others have no regard for you. If green is the colour of jealousy and bile, it is also the colour of nausea, when you are sickened by injustice. Do we need a bit of envy to help us right wrongs?

————•◆•————

This question of whether envy can ever be a virtue is where I turn to John the Baptist. He was one of the greatest moral crusaders of the first century and possibly of all time, and he apparently feels no envy (at least not towards Jesus). This makes him seem rather unreal. He and Jesus were competitors, in a sense. John had a following to rival Jesus' following. He was immensely popular with the crowds who would flock to the desert from Jerusalem to see him. But when Jesus comes along he gives way to him totally. He even gives Jesus some of his own disciples. And all this without a grudging bone in his body. Is this too good to be true?

Of course, the gospel writers are concerned to show that John and Jesus are on the same side. They wouldn't want to suggest any animosity between the two of them. But it is a shame to be cynical about this, as though no one could really be so generous-spirited as John. Such cynicism is itself a sign of envy, of wanting John to fail. Envy is so endemic among us that we feel suspicious of a person who, when their competitor overtakes them, can smile without gritting their teeth. Perhaps we would prefer to see people succumb to envy than conquer it.

Envy is mean-spirited. It is captured in the dictum, it is not enough that you succeed, others have got to fail. It is an actor or a writer who is stung by a colleague getting good reviews, it is a student who feels a pang when a friend does well in finals, it is feeling cut up about someone else's success in securing a job. It is sibling rivalry, and it is warring with people who do not deserve your bitterness. John Chrysostom, who was Bishop of Constantinople at the beginning of the fifth century, described envy as fighting with your brother although he has done you no wrong. And worse still, this all happens under the cloak of friendship. 'Let's go out to the field', Cain says to Abel; and Abel follows in good faith, having no idea that Cain intends to kill him. That is why Abel is remembered in Jewish and Christian tradition as the innocent victim.

Chrysostom said that instead of disposing of his brother, Cain should have let Abel live, and tried to outstrip him in honour. I suppose that competitiveness can channel envy constructively, though it can also exacerbate envious feelings. It may be a solution to certain types of envy, such as envy at another's academic or career success, or indeed their sporting prowess. But it does not answer Cain's problem, not if his problem is one of injustice.

I would advise Cain differently, and suggest not that he compete with Abel but that he have it out with God instead. This might sound evasive or hopelessly other-worldly, but in Cain's case it is the only direct course of action. If anyone had done Cain wrong it was God, not Abel. Therefore Cain should have taken his grievance to God. Then he would have been more like Job who, knowing his suffering was undeserved, demanded an audience with the Almighty. Job grew in moral stature, whereas Cain became a murderer, making his brother pay for his feelings of humiliation. It is often said that oppression breeds oppression, and this happens when people who are ill-treated take out their misery on an innocent third party – usually people who are unwitting, or weak or poor; people who are defenceless. Abel was defenceless because he trusted his brother, and suspected nothing when he went into the field with him. Imagine if John the Baptist had taken against Jesus in a similar way, and held his head under water too long when baptizing him.

If God's behaviour towards Cain was arbitrary, that problem needed tackling at source. (If we have suffered unjustly, let us pray for the courage to go to the people responsible, rather than hitting out at the innocent and unsuspecting.) If it was not arbitrary, Cain would understand that only by allowing God to show him why his offering was rejected. Either way, he needed an audience with God. This is not an evasive tactic. It is one of the hardest things to do because it requires great openness and honesty on our part, to let God show us the truth about ourselves. But once we know that God knows us and still protects us, we do not have to be afraid. When Cain finally spoke with God, he discovered that even after all his crimes God would go on protecting him. He need not have feared. I expect John had to struggle with God when Jesus came along, and the struggle will have made him a better person. For John had reached the point where he stopped fearing his own disappearance, and therefore had no need to begrudge or hurt anyone else. The loss of all fear is the loss of all envy, and is the freedom to rejoice with those who are rejoicing, rather than resent their good news.

———•◆•———

For reflection

1 What would you advise Cain to do when his offering is rejected by God?
2 How have you felt when you have been treated disfavourably for no apparent reason? How have you responded to such disfavour, and how do you wish you had responded?
3 Where have you seen oppression breed oppression? Where have you seen injustice tackled well?
4 Is competitiveness ever a good thing?
5 How do you feel most assured of God's love and protection? How can you extend that certainty into all of your life?

8

Reacting to exclusion

Mark 7.24–37

When a Gentile woman with a needy daughter comes to Jesus, he as good as calls her a dog and refuses at first to help her.

In my experience of reading this passage in Bible studies or with groups of students, men tend to interpret this story differently from women. More often than not, men say that Jesus was testing the Syrophoenician woman, and that he rewarded her when she made a good response. On this reading, Jesus remains all-knowing, and all-good, and fully in control of the situation. By contrast, women more usually read the story from the Syrophoenician woman's perspective, seeing her not as a pawn in one of Jesus' riddles, but as somebody who caused Jesus to change his mind when she told him that even the 'dogs' under the table eat the children's crumbs.

The passage presents us with a double-sided challenge: first, to recognize how we discriminate against others; and second, to learn to respond to our own exclusion. Here is where the Syrophoenician woman can help us. People identify with her most strongly when they are themselves put down or excluded. I expect we can all identify with her in some way, because we have probably all felt rejected at times, if not because of our race or gender, then because of our age, our looks, our accents or our social standing. Being judged and rejected is not an unusual experience at all. We dish out and receive back this kind of treatment all the time.

Religious people ought to be above this kind of thing, but they are not. Part of the explanation (though not an excuse) for the bad behaviour of the 'godly' is that religious systems can set up the most powerful of taboos. This is because they try to protect what they value as holy. The dominant Jewish view in Jesus' day was that God's holiness must be protected from pollution or uncleanness. The Jewish people were ranked according to how pure they were. Women were considered less pure than men, and Gentiles were commonly called 'dogs', which shows that they were viewed with disdain and disgust. This is not so different from Luther calling the Jews 'pigs', or the Nazis likening Jews to rats.

Many of the Jewish purity laws were of course to do with food, because what could be more polluting than ingesting something unclean? Compare the situation in India today where, despite legislation, the lowest caste of people are still regarded as untouchable. The 'untouchables' are forbidden to let even their eating utensils come into contact with the kitchen utensils of higher castes.

Bizarre experiments in probing the boundaries of disgust were carried out in a recent television series *Anatomy of Disgust,* shown on Channel 4. Cakes made of tasty ingredients but looking like faeces were offered to children. They were gladly accepted by the two-year-olds, but rejected by those over the age of four. A cap that had been worn by a Nazi guard was placed on a kitchen table, and students were offered biscuits that had been brushed against it. No one could bring themselves to eat them. The sense that you will be defiled by eating something unclean is very strong. So we can imagine the impact Jesus must have made when he said it is not what you eat that defiles you, but what comes from inside. This was the statement Jesus made just before he encountered the Syrophoenician woman.

Except for his initial knee-jerk reaction to this woman, Jesus took extreme risks in cutting through the system of taboos that defined his own culture. He pulled down barriers physically, by touch. Look at the intimate way he dealt with the deaf man after his encounter with the Syrophoenician woman. He put his fingers into the man's ears and spat. Saliva was considered unclean, as we can understand – we think it unclean ourselves. It is not clear why Jesus spat, but he touched the deaf man's tongue and may even have mingled the man's saliva with his own to bring about the cure. In any case, it was by intimate physical contact that he ended the man's deafness and also his isolation. Some of the things Jesus did, like going into a tomb, or having contact with lepers, would have caused a visceral reaction of revulsion because of fear of contagion. It would be the kind of reaction people still sometimes make on discovering that they are sharing a kitchen, or bathroom, or communion cup with someone who is living with AIDS.

Jesus reintegrated people into society by physically and socially engaging with them. When we shake hands with people, or share food with them, or sit with them, it is almost impossible at the same time to regard them as dogs, or pigs or rats. We humanize others by engaging with them, and at the same time we humanize ourselves. The inverse is also true. The people we won't shake hands with are the people we bestialize, and we turn ourselves into beasts in the process.

The smallest bit of contact can have big effects. I was recently walking home after a wedding when three homeless men stopped me because I was wearing a dog-collar. We chatted for about five minutes, shook hands, and as I was leaving they said: 'Thank you for talking to us, and thank you for encouraging us.' I was very struck, because I hadn't said anything encouraging to them. In fact we had talked about night clubs! But if you are used to people walking by and ignoring you as though you don't exist, someone stopping to talk is itself an encouragement.

———— •◆• ————

The challenge posed by the problem of exclusion is two-sided. It is not just about how we should include others, but about how to respond when others exclude us.

In the year 2000, the Pope reiterated the official stance of the Vatican that Anglican churches and all Protestant churches are 'defective'. Anglicans especially do not like this because (speaking as an Anglican) we regard ourselves as truly Catholic (while also being Reformed), and as being in the line of apostolic succession. But the Vatican holds that we are not truly part of the 'one, holy, Catholic and apostolic Church'; that our churches are not 'proper' churches, and that our communion in Christ is 'imperfect'. Rome's concern, of course, is to protect divine truth and God's holiness, and so she has a kind of purity code that excludes us.

Anglicans flinch to be classed by Rome as also-rans. And yet Rome's attitude towards Anglicans resembles Anglican attitudes towards nonconformist and independent churches in Britain. They respond to us rather well, I think (again, speaking as an Anglican), and rather as the Syrophoenician woman did to Jesus. I was part of a group convened after Lambeth 1998, to try to improve Anglican relations with Pentecostal churches. The Anglican tendency, as always, was to think that we must set the terms of acceptance. But a Black Pentecostal Bishop soon put us right: 'Pentecostals have done it themselves', he said. 'How do you engage with people who have done it themselves, without you?' Like the Syrophoenician woman, he was saying, we Black Pentecostals are already participating in the life of God, and enjoying God's blessings. He also said that if we wanted to work with them in their mission to the poor, they'd be glad to have us. But if we want to sit around discussing what we all have in common, they are too busy! Fair enough; I thought this was a good response. The Syrophoenician woman would not have wanted to sit around discussing her credentials with the Jews. She had a daughter to get healed.

The Black Pentecostal Bishop has not turned his back on Anglicans. The Syrophoenician woman did not turn her back on Jesus. She kept her faith that the power of God is at work in Jesus, even when she was rebuffed. She did not have an inferiority complex. She stood her ground, and she saw the mismatch between Jesus' reaction to her, and the kind of God about whom Jesus spoke.

We are forever being exhorted to recognize and overcome our prejudices. But while asking ourselves, 'How do we exclude others?', we should also ask, 'How do we react when others exclude us?' If we can stand our ground like the Syrophoenician woman did, believing that God does not reject us, we can resist people's efforts to regard us as sub-human. We can also save others from turning themselves into beasts by their own bigotry. On the interpretation I favour, the Syrophoenician woman gave Jesus a wake-up call when she told him that the 'dogs' are eating the children's food from underneath the table.

For reflection

1 Which character do you most identify with in the story of Jesus' encounter with the Syrophoenician woman? Do you find the story disturbing in any way?
2 Have you had experience of being regarded as unsuitable, or of not belonging?
3 How might a rejected person respond, in light of this story?
4 What can we learn from Jesus' change of tone towards the woman: 'For saying that, you may go – the demon has left your daughter'?
5 How might we best react when our own prejudices are pointed out to us?

9

Christ and the Temple

Luke 2.22–40

Jesus begins his life in obedience to the Temple, but ends his life in defiance of it. It is in the Temple that he is first recognized as the salvation of the world. But the Temple is set to become a point of struggle for him. He is carried and tempted there by the devil (Luke 4.9), and when he arrives in Jerusalem for the final time to die, the Temple is his main place of conflict.

The Temple did temporarily overwhelm Jesus. It was a huge institution, much bigger than him, and it crushed him. And yet he had in many ways been obedient to the Temple, brought up in its system and with a sense of allegiance to it. Moreover, at the end of Luke's gospel, and at the beginning of the Book of Acts, we see Jesus' disciples praying and teaching there. Theirs is the struggle between staying and going: when to be part of a system and when to let go.

This was no small matter. The Temple was the place that gave identity to the people of God. It maintained the entire system of holiness laws that related Israel to God, and the people to one another. These laws enabled careful avoidance of contact with anything impure or unholy. Jesus' mother came to the Temple to be purified 40 days after giving birth, because according to Levitical law a mother was impure in the flow of her blood until she had been through such a rite (Leviticus 12).

In fact, Luke conflates two temple rites: the purification of the mother, and the offering of the first-born son. He might have been confused about Jewish custom. But the beauty of it is that he has Jesus' parents redeeming Jesus from the Lord God, literally buying him back, making a sacrifice to the Lord so that they can keep their son. So the Redeemer is redeemed. Moreover, he is redeemed by the simple, rude sacrifice of two pigeons, which marked his family out as being poor. The offering of birds was made by those who could not afford a lamb.

As an adult, Jesus fell foul of this very system of Temple purity. Once on his public ministry, he started offending it at almost every turn. Under this system it was utterly shocking that he associated with sinners and lepers, the blind and lame, tax-collectors, prostitutes, adulterers, Samaritans, Gentiles, bleeding women and corpses. These were dirty. He was tainting himself.

The American writer Maya Angelou recalls being taken as a child screaming with toothache to a dentist, and the dentist refusing to treat her, saying, 'I'd rather stick my hand in a dog's mouth than in a nigger's.' That is the sort of attitude Jesus was challenging. Actually, it is stronger than an 'attitude'. It is a very physical response of disgust. It is the sort of reaction we make to disease-carrying animals, such as rats or rabid dogs, because we are afraid of being contaminated by them. We wouldn't want to put our hands near their mouths, and the thought of eating them would make us retch.

Jesus cut through the whole system of taboos that defined Jewish culture in his day. When he healed people he did not just cure them physically, but made them well in their relationships with others. By touching and engaging with them, he removed their stigma and shame, and reintegrated them into society. He was charged with 'perverting the nation', which is the kind of thing Christian Right activists say in America about people who are too accepting of others. His actions and his words declared that people are pure or impure in God's sight according to what is inside them, not according to what their bodies are like, and not according to what they eat. By tackling the food laws he cut right to the heart of our fears of contamination by challenging us not only to associate with 'unclean' people but to ingest food that had been declared 'unclean':

> He said to them, 'Then do you also fail to understand? Do you not see that whatever goes into a person from outside cannot defile, since it enters, not the heart but the stomach, and goes out into the sewer?' (Thus he declared all foods clean.) And he said, 'It is what comes out of a person that defiles. For it is from within, from the human heart, that evil intentions come.' (Mark 7.18–21)

Given Jesus' radical challenges to the Temple, what should we make of the fact that he was obedient to it in many ways, and that the first Christians maintained their links with it? Did they struggle to show allegiance and to stay within a system that had contributed to Jesus' death? I imagine their dilemmas were quite similar to ones many people feel about the Church; believing in the Church's authority, and loving the Church in many ways, but finding that they keep tripping over barriers they don't think should be there. I wouldn't be surprised if all people in the Church feel like this in one way or another.

Nancy Eiesland is a theologian in a wheelchair. She describes the Church as a 'City on a hill': physically inaccessible and socially inhospitable. She calls people without disabilities the 'temporarily able-bodied', to remind us that our abilities are not permanent and that none of us can be set apart as perfect. When you think about this, and then consider the Levitical laws about who could approach the altar, the exclusivity of those laws is quite astounding. The Lord instructed Moses to tell Aaron that: 'no one who has a blemish shall draw near, one who is blind or lame, or one who has a mutilated face or a limb too long, or one who has a broken foot or a broken hand, or a hunchback, or a dwarf, or a man with a blemish in his eyes or an itching disease or scabs or crushed testicles' (Leviticus 21.18–20). One translation says the short-sighted cannot come near, so what hope is there for any of us? To understand that we are at most temporarily able-bodied connects us to the rest of humanity. Why draw barriers?

When we realize our connectedness, we can be in solidarity with one another: the kind of solidarity Christ showed by becoming a human being like us and suffering the consequences. At the point where he identified with us most deeply, he was not unblemished and able-bodied, and he was not at all socially acceptable. He was marked and disabled by being flogged and pinned on a cross, losing the power of his arms and legs. His was a broken and disgraced body, and he died like a criminal. But he did not resist being identified with the maimed and shamed, and he turned out to have God on his side. It was what happened after his death that ultimately overturned the Temple system for Christians. Jesus' state by the time he was dead was in every way abhorrent to that system, but it turned out that he was not abhorrent to God.

For reflection

1 Do we have anything resembling the Jewish purity laws in our ways of categorizing people today?
2 Do people ever become better by being excluded, or by excluding others?
3 What kind of change was Jesus trying to bring about in his society?
4 Has the Church continued Jesus' work?
5 Do people experience our churches as exclusive? Have we experienced exclusion? What can we do about exclusive tendencies in church?

10

Incarnation and shame

Titus 2.1–8, 11–14

The letter to Titus contains commands for various members of a household. The only one that raises a smile for me is the instruction to women not to be slanderers and slaves to drink. I have no desire to be either of those things, but something about the rest of the injunctions makes me want to say: 'Way to go, girls. Get drunk and swear. I'm glad to think you were doing that in first-century Crete', which is where Titus' community lived.

The other injunctions that come in the letter to Titus knock the wind out of me, and deaden my spirit. This is because whenever there are lists of how men and women should behave, it is always implied that men are closer to God than women. Women are made strange: different beings, at one remove from where the real business with God is happening. How can I praise God if I am humiliated in God's house? How can we praise the Lord in a strange land?

The implication that women are somewhat removed from God has set me thinking about the many people who are held at arm's length just because of the way they are, and the multitudes of people who are alienated and persecuted because of what their bodies are like. The world is full of such people. I mean those whose very being, their enfleshed, incarnate selves, is held against them. Anyone who doesn't fit because they've got the wrong colour hair, or the wrong colour skin, or the wrong chromosomes, or the wrong hormones, or the wrong body shape or formation, or quite frankly the wrong parentage, will know what I mean. Surely there are some of you reading this, otherwise I'm in very rarefied company!

You may have seen Britain's favourite talkshow host Michael Parkinson interview America's most prized talkshow host Oprah Winfrey, shortly after she had appeared in a film about slaves in

America. Parkinson asked her about her struggles as a black woman, but she turned the questions on him. 'Tell me,' she said, 'do you feel privileged as a white man?' He said he did in a way, and she said, 'Yes, because you are able to move through the world without encountering any obstacles.' (Having money is also a factor in enjoying this kind of freedom!) Winfrey here gives us a very helpful image. There are no places that Parkinson and men like him cannot go. The world is not a strange place to them. This is a privilege, and I wish that more people would use it well. It is open to just a fraction of the world's population.

By contrast, encountering obstacles to our being is not an unusual experience at all, and it is one that eats away at our self-respect and makes us feel ashamed. In the Church, the issues over women's ordination and homosexuality are very physical matters. Very often, people who disagree on these matters are unable to face one another, literally, and so they look away, or cast their eyes to the ground, or turn their backs on one another. The sheer physicality of the issues is even clearer when worshippers flinch from sharing the Peace, or from touching holy objects that they feel have been 'tainted' by an unclean hand. It is explicit in churches that believe a woman priest can defile a sanctuary or pollute the hands of the bishop who ordains her. People's incarnate nature is made cause for their shame.

———— • ◆ • ————

I was recently invited to discuss with the Women's Committee of a student union the question, 'Can you be religious and a feminist?'. Several Jewish, Christian, Muslim and Sikh women were there, defending their faith as compatible with feminism. They argued that by going back to the original scriptures of their various faiths, they could show that at the very source and heart of their faiths there is good news for women. This meant interpreting the story of Adam and Eve in such a way that Eve does not come off badly, and interpreting injunctions on women's behaviour as really being to women's advantage, and so on. But this left me wondering: what happens to your faith when the scriptures are not okay, and when no amount of interpretation can justify the attitudes they sanction about women? We need to be honest about what has been handed down to us in scripture, and not gloss over the difficult bits, or pretend that they are nicer than they seem.

When the time first came round for me to preach on the biblical teaching, 'wives be submissive to your husbands', it was from this particular passage in the letter to Titus. Some people would choose not to follow the lectionary at this point, and go with a different reading; but as I have said, we do need to face up to our biblical heritage. However, on this occasion the lectionary itself was not being upfront. It missed out a few verses in the middle of the passage. We should read them anyway. Our ears are not too delicate to hear them or our minds to apprehend them. They go like this: 'Tell slaves to be submissive to their masters and to give satisfaction in every respect; they are not to answer back, not to pilfer, but to show complete and perfect fidelity, so that in everything they may be an ornament to the doctrine of God our saviour' (Titus 2.9–10).

Why did the lectionary compilers omit these words? Did they feel ashamed by them? Do commands to slaves offend our cultural sensibilities? Are they unbecoming of the Gospel? Why else exclude them? But then why include the injunctions on women? Both come out of the same cultural context, where there were extended households with particular authority structures. Our living arrangements are not like those of Titus' community, and so this passage is a dud one for us. It is like a bell without resonance. Yet people persist in trying to make it resonate.

In our culture, the teaching that wives submit to their husbands has squeezed people into relationships that are just not real for them. This can have a comical side. For example, it is quite typical of a number of churches today to have women pastors holding authority on church matters but submitting to their husbands at home. In church he does as she says, but in the household 'he reigns', as several pastors have put it to me. How odd to divide your life up like that, and to demarcate something so fluid as a marriage. The idea that women can have authority over men anywhere but in the home is peculiar to our time, and rather ironic!

But this isn't simply funny. It can have very grave consequences. The pressure on women to submit to their husbands has made it easy for women to be blamed when things go wrong. ('You shouldn't have worn so short a skirt' syndrome.) This is at its most serious when wives are being abused; and statistics show that domestic abuse is rife in strict religious households. Some churches today use this teaching to encourage battered wives to bear with it and wait on

God to reform their husbands. Not surprisingly, women can come to believe that their beatings reflect a failure on their own part to be sufficiently godly. They can come to believe that they deserve what they get. Holly Wagner Green wrote of her experience as a battered wife, and the counselling she received from others in her church:

> 'You shouldn't leave your husband' one woman said to her, 'No matter what he does to you, God put him in charge of you. He's God's responsibility. If something he does to you displeases God, then it's up to God to stop him, not you.' 'That's right', another woman added, 'God made him your lord and master. Even if he tells you to jump out of the window, you should do it. If God wants you or your baby to live, don't worry. He'll protect you somehow.'

This example is extreme, but sadly not uncommon. Of course, the problem here is less with scripture than with the way that scripture is used. But that is always the case. The Bible itself does not go around harming people. It's dynamic, but it can't do anything on its own. Without us it doesn't have limbs. What scripture can do, for good or ill, depends on what we do with scripture. Where it is used oppressively, rather than for our liberation, this is something close to blasphemy. But a liberative use of scripture must involve arguing with those portions that seem to support injustice. This is itself a biblical thing to do: it is the voice of the prophets who cried for mercy rather than sacrifice, and of Abraham who argued with God to save Sodom and Gomorrah, and of Jacob who wrestled with God. It is the voice of Job, who demanded that God vindicate him against the religious ethos of his day, which held that Job deserved his suffering. It is second nature to Black-led churches in Britain, whose experience of the Holy Spirit convinces them to denounce biblical injunctions on slaves. By appealing directly to God, they judge as un-Christian any text or institution that would condone slavery.

Teaching on wifely submission weds women to practices that are not good for them by making women submit to their husbands rather than directly to God. When a Christian community looks on in silence at a wife being battered in her home, this is a direct result of the conviction that men are answerable to God but women are answerable to men, or as Milton wrote in *Paradise Lost,* 'he for God only, she for God in him'. When women are held at one remove from God like this, they know shame, because their self-respect is undermined.

This is not the same as shame that we have earned by being wilfully committed to the wrong thing. When shame is properly our own, it can be the turning point for our repentance and redemption. But when we are made to carry the consequences of someone else's wrongdoing, made to wear a star of David or a pink triangle on our sleeve, not given a seat on a bus or forbidden entry into the sanctuary, the shame does us no good at all. It wears us down and empties us of self-respect. This is why Pride has become politically important, as with Black Pride and Gay Pride. It is one way of reclaiming an integrity of being. It is also why people try to discover how to be Christlike in such circumstances, for Christ maintained dignity through suffering, and promised the Holy Spirit to help us. But this is the more painful path because it keeps us vulnerable, as we try to practise loving our enemies. Vulnerability can be a strength if it prevents us becoming brittle and fragile, and enables us to receive God's love so that we can give love. But it must be combined with the knowledge that our very being is in the image of God, and that God has not looked down upon our flesh.

Christ's Incarnation was God's glory being shown on earth. It was also Christ's suffering, and it was not pretty: beaten and hung on the cross to die, probably naked and after some rough handling by soldiers. But the shame he bore was not properly his. He did not earn it. It belonged to his persecutors and executioners, and to those who withdrew their friendship. He took his petitions to God alone, who did not dishonour him. God does not hold us at arm's length, but dignifies us. We are called forth in love by our Creator who owns us without shame.

For reflection

1 What does it mean to be Christlike when you are subjected to violence?
2 Are you aware of people suffering because of the way that others regard them? How might we respond to the shame this causes?
3 Should wives, or husbands, put up with anything in order to stay together?
4 Is pride sometimes a virtue?
5 How can we respond to biblical teachings that seem very distant from our own age?

11

Widows

Mark 12.38–44

In the hubbub of the Temple, Jesus draws attention to a widow who passes by unassumingly. He does not speak to her, nor personally commend her for her extravagance. But he picks her out for special comment, and this must have challenged the way his disciples thought about things, for she was a poor, vulnerable woman, unattractive to society and almost entirely beyond notice.

It is the little people, in Mark's gospel, who exemplify the values that Jesus teaches. They have fleeting cameo appearances, but their roles are memorable. Think of the woman who anointed Jesus' feet. She is involved in only that one brief episode, but Jesus says, 'I tell you, wherever the good news is proclaimed in all the world, what she has done will be told in memory of her' (Mark 14.9). Think also of the Syrophoenician woman, of Jairus, and of Joseph of Arimathaea. They are 'the little ones who have faith' (to use Jesus' way of speaking). Unlike the blundering disciples and the uncomprehending crowds, it is they who live out the values that Jesus preaches. As characters in the story, their role resembles the role of Christ: they are people in whom we can see the things of God.

How surprised are we by this? On one level we become rather used to Jesus shattering our preconceptions, and turning our standards upside down. We're not surprised to find Christ identifying with the poor and arguing with the élite. But on a more practical level, we are just as hopeless ourselves at grasping Jesus' message as were the unbelieving crowds who obstructed his ministry. We do not really take on board that a poor widow, one of society's unimportant and forgotten people, can represent Christ. We have not really learned that she is someone in whom we see the things of God, and that she is the sort of person we should try to be like.

What is it to have our preconceptions shattered? Church market-ing campaigns have gone off in an irrelevant direction at this point. They focus on shattering people's image of church, of Christ, and of what Christians are like. They seem to want to say: Christ is radically hip, and his groupies know how to have a good time. A Christian night club called 'Abundant' has opened in London, and it makes a virtue of drinking and swearing and staging kiss 'n' tell evenings. I am all for Christians going clubbing if they want to, but there is no Gospel message in it. Showing that Christians can drink and swear and be promiscuous (or even pretend to be promiscuous) is all about wanting to improve the image of Christians. It is too self-orientated and self-conscious, and it plays into the very value-systems that the Church ought to be subverting. The poor widow would most likely pass by the front door of 'Abundant' without being noticed, just as she passed through the Temple unnoticed until Jesus pointed her out. There is nothing about her that is attractive to youth culture. There is nothing about her that is attractive to anyone, except those concerned with the values of God's kingdom. The preconceptions that need challenging are not people's views about Christians, but their understanding of where God's favour lies. If Christians took care of this, their own image would look after itself.

Bible stories about poor and powerless people show us that God has a particular concern for those who are vulnerable. God knows full well what a rotten life widows have when they have no protector and are dependent on charity. God knows there is no level playing-field, and looks kindly on those who are the least advantaged. God's commendation of people is not to do with who is 'chosen', in the sense of being an Israelite or a follower of Christ. After all, the poor widow in the Temple had no contact with Jesus. She had not walked with him or sat at his feet. The two probably never met, but she exemplifies his message.

———•◆•———

Similarly, another famous widow in our scriptures (1 Kings 17), the widow who helped Elijah, did not worship Elijah's God. She was a Sidonian, a heathen. Yet she served the prophet as God's people had failed to do. She treated Elijah according to the godly values by which the Israelites were themselves supposed to live, particularly by showing hospitality to a stranger, and giving food and water to one who is hungry. Here is her story:

> [Elijah] set out and went to Zarephath. When he came to the gate of the town, a widow was there gathering sticks; he called to her and said, 'Bring me a little water in a vessel, so that I may drink.' As she was going to bring it, he called to her and said, 'Bring me a morsel of bread in your hand.' But she said, 'As the Lord your God lives, I have nothing baked, only a handful of meal in a jar, and a little oil in a jug; I am now gathering a couple of sticks, so that I may go home and prepare it for myself and my son, that we may eat it, and die.' Elijah said to her, 'Do not be afraid; go and do as you have said; but first make me a little cake of it and bring it to me, and afterwards make something for yourself and your son. For thus says the Lord the God of Israel: The jar of meal will not be emptied and the jug of oil will not fail until the day that the Lord sends rain on the earth.' She went and did as Elijah said, so that she as well as he and her household ate for many days. The jar of meal was not emptied, neither did the jug of oil fail, according to the word of the Lord that he spoke by Elijah. (1 Kings 17.10–16)

She, like the widow whom Jesus spotted in the Temple, got it right.

But what exactly did these women get right? It is easy for us to think that we know the message of these stories. We read them in a familiar framework and make ourselves comfortable with them. If we are really to be challenged by them, we need to let them shake us up. A friend tells me that the story of the widow's mite used to make her cry as a child because she felt sorry for the widow having nothing left to live on. It is a shocking story: how can it be good that the poor widow gave all she had? Her money was not even going to a particularly needy cause. It went into the Temple coffers, which were presumably already quite full. Think of the dangers of cultic attitudes in religious groups the world over, where quite impoverished people are encouraged to give, even when to do so means not having enough money to get through the rest of the week. In a television documentary about one particular cult, a woman being interviewed described how members of her cult demanded the $5-note from her purse, even though it was the only money she had to buy milk for her baby. She was pressured into giving the money with the promise that she would receive more back in return. Is this like the self-replenishing flask of oil awarded to the widow who took the food from her son's mouth in order to feed Elijah?

The woman on television felt angry and exploited. What made the act of giving wrong for her but right for Elijah's widow? It was not as though Elijah had asked nicely! If I were that widow, I think I would feel very put upon by Elijah's command that I feed him before feeding my own offspring, and I would want to defend a mother's first loyalty to her children and to her own well-being. I worry about extolling the selflessness of both Elijah's widow and the widow in the Temple, because selflessness is something that vulnerable women, especially mothers, practise quite proficiently. Many could do with feeling less guilty about looking after themselves.

So I find the stories of the widows uncomfortable and undomesticated. Even if we treat them as parables rather than as actual incidents, they still need translating into action, and I am wary about that. The women gave extravagantly. Their acts were hugely costly: one took food from her starving son, the other gave all she had to live on. Are these the demands of the kingdom?

It helps, I think, to see that the widow whom Elijah approached had a very specific request made to her, and by someone who was himself hungry. She was in an extreme situation, which required extreme and courageous acts, and she understood what she needed to do. Her act of giving should not be held up as an absolute good, but as a response to God in specific circumstances. The lesson for us is not necessarily to do as she did, but to respond to God out of our own situations, some of which will require actions just as risky and demanding.

The stories of the widows are not about demands so much as responses. Jesus said the kingdom of heaven is like a treasure for which it is worth giving up everything (Matthew 13.44). The rich young ruler was not able to part with his wealth (Matthew 19). The poor widow was. Both had known something of God's goodness and love, but one responded more fully than the other, because she held nothing back. Holding nothing back is our fitting response to God.

What does this mean for us? What it means in detail will vary according to our circumstances and calling: it meant something different for each of the widows, and something different again for Peter, and for Paul, and for Mary Magdalene. It means something different for Sheila Cassidy and for Desmond Tutu and for each one of us.

But whatever our own personal costs, if we are to live as people whom Jesus commends, we must learn to sit lightly to everything we might have to give up, to our possessions, to our self-image, to social respect, to our livelihoods. Then we will have understood that living in response to God is worth more than all these, and we will be little people in whom, hopefully, others will see something of God.

————— ◆ —————

For reflection

1 Why did Jesus commend the poor widow for what she gave to the Temple? How should we try to be like her?
2 Do you feel differently about giving to the Church than about giving to charity?
3 Have you or people you know been challenged to give up the money you depend on? If so, how did you or they respond? Where was God in that situation?
4 Have we become more concerned with the image of Christianity than with living as Christ taught us to live?
5 How are you being asked to respond to God?

12

Preparing to meet our maker

Luke 6.17–26

Do we fall on the wrong side of this gospel passage? Are we the rich and well-fed, the laughing people who enjoy good standing among our neighbours? Or are we people who are hungry now, or weeping now, or people who are hated and reviled? Jesus' blessings and woes restore a social balance between the 'haves' and 'have-nots'. Most of us who are born in the developed world have enough food and a roof over our heads. We are 'haves', most of us. So is Jesus pronouncing woes on us? And if he is, what should we do about it?

To a large extent, our circumstances are what we might call a matter of luck. When I say 'luck', I don't mean to speak irreligiously. I am using the philosophical idea of moral luck, which describes people being blamed and praised for things that are not entirely their own doing. For example, if you are in the right place at the right time to save a child from wandering into the road, you may well be held up as a hero. If you are in the wrong place at the wrong time, you could be unlucky enough to drive into that child and be cast as a villain. Are we cast as villains by Jesus' words because we have the 'ill luck' of living comfortably in a prosperous society? Does material good fortune count against us in God's eyes?

We should not try to make Jesus' words palatable by softening them in some way. We cannot in all honesty spiritualize these sayings of Jesus because Luke makes them very physical, very personal, and very immediate: 'Blessed are you who are hungry now, for you will be filled.' It was Matthew who put it differently: 'Blessed are those who hunger and thirst for righteousness.' Luke was concerned with material poverty.

The novelist and religious critic A. N. Wilson is alarmed at Jesus' vehemence. He thinks Jesus had a very damning attitude, and he says he cannot admire anyone who went around pronouncing woes on people. But to understand Jesus' words, we have to see that they fit a particular genre. This was how the prophets spoke. 'Woe to him who builds his house by unrighteousness, and his upper rooms by injustice; who makes his neighbours work for nothing, and does not give them their wages' (Jeremiah 22.13). There was a whole tradition that Jesus drew upon, of pronouncing woes on people who are well off, and who cannot see outside their own windows. The message was one of justice. It was given as a warning to the complacent and an encouragement to the poor and downtrodden. It is not a message that either rich or poor should receive passively, but one that should inspire and activate change.

So what should we do in response to the gospel? Should we renounce our riches? I'm not sure. Luke does not celebrate poverty, he celebrates the poor having their fill. He is not promoting the ascetic life. After all, he wrote his gospel and the Book of Acts to churches around the Mediterranean that were not impoverished. These churches met in private houses big enough to accommodate them. Moreover, the Apostle Paul – who was Luke's big hero – boasted that he was a man of independent means. There were many people among Luke's friends and contacts who socially must have been rather like averagely affluent Westerners.

I am not trying to soften the gospel message: I'm trying to understand it. The reason we should not feel comfortable in the present time is not because comfort is bad in itself, but because all is not well with the world. It is wrong to feel at ease in a situation that is not all right.

Let me try putting it this way. If you should find yourself thinking, 'I wish people would stop rocking the boat', ask yourself why. Probably it is because you are comfortable in the boat, and you don't see why others should make waves. But turbulence starts when not everyone is having a fair time of it. In fact, scores of people may be outside the boat and drowning. We are not right to feel comfortable in any situation that is distressing to others. Jesus afflicts the comfortable so that they might do something to comfort the afflicted. The American theologian Don Browning says that if we have riches and privileges, this does not make us more sinful, for sin affects everyone, but it may indeed make us more guilty. This is because the more riches and privileges people have, the nearer they are to seats of wealth and power, and therefore the more possibilities they have for bringing about change.

———— •◆• ————

Sometimes it takes a stripping down process, where you face losing everything, or discover that even those closest to you cannot support you, before you realize your need of God. God is ultimately the one who is left supporting us. If we can understand that, we can move through this world with a kind of freedom – without the need to cling on to things, to people, or to reputation. While material comfort and an easy route through life can make us complacent, loss and shake-up can actually bring us freedom.

Paul had to wrestle with the Christians in Corinth over their complacency. Their problem was that they thought they already shared Christ's glory. For this reason, they did not believe in the resurrection of the dead (1 Corinthians 15.12). They were comfortable now, and so had no hopes beyond this world. Paul corrects them: 'If for this life only we have hoped in Christ,' he says, 'we are of all people most to be pitied' (vs 19).

But why should we be pitied if we focus on this life? There are philosophers of religion at present who are saying just the opposite. They hold that the whole way of thinking in the West, from the time of Plato onwards, has been far too fixated with death. They mean that we have been obsessed with sacrifice and violence, and with freeing the soul from the confines of the body and gaining eternal life, when instead we should focus on birth, and hope and our lives in this world. (If you are interested in following this up, see Grace Jantzen's volume *Becoming Divine*. The details are given at the end of this book.)

Along the same lines, somebody asked me once why we make so much of Jesus defeating death rather than evil. After all, she said, death is not the worst thing that can happen. And she is right; some ravages of evil are worse than some deaths, and some deaths have a peace about them. We need to know that Jesus overcame evil.

But while death may not be the worse thing that could happen to us, it is the ultimate thing. If we overcome evil, but not death, we still have to face death, and what would we face it with? But if we are conquerors of death, who can stop us from fighting evil?

People who have lost the fear of death are a big threat to society because nothing intimidates them. If death does not deter them, then nothing else will either, and so they have the power to do great harm or great good. We know about the harm, because we know about suicide bombers and about people who are prepared to fly aircraft into buildings. In the aftermath of 11 September 2001, when the World Trade Center and Pentagon in America were struck by hijacked passenger planes, Richard Dawkins asserted in the *Guardian* newspaper that religion devalues life because it 'teaches the dangerous nonsense that death is not the end'. The hi-jackers were Muslim martyrs who believed they would go straight to paradise.

Richard Dawkins is Professor of the Public Understanding of Science in Oxford, and a self-professed and very public enemy of religion. He says that by religion, testosterone-sodden young men can be suckered into believing that by flying a plane into a skyscraper they will be put on a fast track to a Great Oasis in the Sky, where they will receive a special martyr's reward of 72 virgin brides. One young man from Finsbury Park Mosque, interviewed on the television news, put it like this: 'The more people we kill, the happier we will be in paradise.'

But there are others who lose the fear of death not primarily because they are looking forward to some nice reward in the afterlife, but because they are so discomfited by injustice that they are prepared even to die in a struggle for justice. And if they die, they do so not only passionately, as suicide bombers do, but compassionately – suffering with others, rather than making others suffer. Martin Luther King had received a number of threats on his life for his efforts to dismantle racism and promote civil rights. In the last speech he ever made, he said this: 'Like anybody, I would like to live a long life. Longevity has its place. But I'm not concerned with that now. I just want to do God's will. And He's allowed me to go up to the mountain. And I've looked over. And I've seen the promised land. I may not get there with you. But . . . we as a people will get to the promised land.' He was shot dead the next day. He realized he might well die for his efforts, but he had lost his fear of death. Such people are not afraid to make colossal waves.

We are wrong to place all our hope in this world, to feel that we have arrived, that we are safe and sound. We are wrong to do this because all is not well with the world. If we are lucky enough to have food, and joy and good social standing, there are many more who aren't. For those of us who live comfortably, it is all too easy to carry on doing so without greatly challenging our lifestyles. Complacency breeds ignorance (an ability to ignore others), and our ignorance is someone else's misery. We might ask ourselves what suffering we have closed our eyes to that we can now begin to see. Jesus rocked the boat not because he was hard-up and socially despised, but because he saw that others were.

―――――•◆•―――――

For reflection

1   Jesus said, 'Woe to you who are rich.' Do you think he was speaking to us?
2   What and whom do you most rely upon in life? Imagine being stripped clean of your possessions and then of your relationships. What and whom would you be most shattered to lose?
3   Do you live comfortably in ways that might dampen your awareness of the needs of others? Do you feel comfortable in ways that perhaps lessen your reliance on God? How might you change?
4   Have you ever felt threatened or irritated by people 'rocking the boat'? Or, have you felt let down by others not joining you in a struggle? How would you now reflect on those situations?
5   Is there anything or anyone you would be prepared to die for?

13

Having the mind of God

Isaiah 55.1–9

Can we ever come to think God's thoughts? The physicist Stephen Hawking has famously said that if we could discover why we and the universe exist, then we would know the mind of God. But the words from Isaiah, 'my thoughts are not your thoughts, nor are your ways my ways, says the Lord', suggest that the mind of God is not something we could discover through physical exploration and philosophical reflection. Having the mind of God is not a matter of knowledge so much as of vision. To think God's thoughts is to envision something that goes beyond what we see around us, and is perhaps contrary to it.

We could feel a bit helpless about this, but the prophet's words in the Book of Isaiah were given to encourage rather than confound us. The gap between our thinking and God's is reassuring in many ways.

Most especially, the passage in Isaiah is about being encouraged by hope when we have no physical evidence of God's blessings. Here, God's 'thoughts' do not mean divine reflections, or lofty super-intelligence, so much as God's plans or purposes. The people of Israel are in exile when these words are given to them. They are weary and resigned. They cannot see God's designs, because there are no visible and tangible signs of them. They look about them and see their oppression. They are a people beaten down and discouraged. But they are invited to come buy and eat, without money and without price. This is something incomprehensible, something we think is impossible. But to think God's thoughts is to lift our faces in hope – the hope that something for which we have no evidence is nonetheless possible.

If we are in a tumultuous time, or have just received bad news, and feel worn down physically and emotionally, we may not see much light on the horizon. Thankfully, this passage from Isaiah does not ask us to see light. That is a relief. It encourages us instead to go by things we cannot see: to believe that there is hope for something better than the wearied and resigned assessments we might make of our own situation.

The poet Philip Larkin once told a journalist that Margaret Thatcher's great strength as Prime Minister was 'saying that two and two make four'. She was hard-nosed in her economics, and realistic about finances. But it takes no vision to state that 2 + 2 = 4: almost anyone can do that sum. As the writer Alan Bennett points out, what Larkin failed to see is that it is only by banking on two and two making five that worthy projects ever get under way. Once you insist that the numbers only add up to four, you start making cuts and closing down projects. To hold open the possibility that two and two could make five is to go beyond realistic assessments: it is to defy the bold facts staring you in the face, and reach out for the possibility of something richer. Visionaries hold out for two and two making five, and they help people to turn their situation around.

The gap between our thoughts and God's is a hopeful one. One way of responding to it is to accept, against the evidence, that no troubles need overcome us. The Apostle Paul told the church in Corinth that 'God is faithful and will not let you be tested beyond your strength, but will also provide the way out' (1 Corinthians 10.13). Paul's teaching was significantly different from secular teaching of the time. For example, the philosopher Seneca, whose brother was proconsul of Achaea at the time of Paul's stay in Corinth, taught that no one can suffer both severely and for a long time, because nature has made us such that our pain is either endurable or short. For that matter, Richard Swinburne, who is one of the most prolific philosophers of religion at the turn of this century, argues essentially the same point as Seneca, though he does so as a Christian. He says that God has put limits to our suffering by making us in such a way that we fall unconscious or die when our suffering would otherwise become unbearable.

These are not Paul's sentiments. Paul is not talking about nature's way of curtailing suffering, but about how God relates to us in our suffering. His point is not that we can either pass out or pass away, as Seneca and Swinburne have said, but that God provides us with the means to endure. So there is in this saying both an assurance and a challenge. The assurance is that God will not let us be overwhelmed. The challenge is to find the way through. This may sometimes mean finding the handle that brings release, but often it means staying put and drawing on God's strength when we have no reserves of our own. Either way, we are called to think beyond our natural state, to the higher thoughts or purposes of God.

———•◆•———

Since there is a gap between God's thoughts and ours, God's revelation remains shocking and strange. God's ways will never be predictable or familiar to us. Part of this strangeness is that Jesus was an enigmatic and very puzzling figure. Even those closest to him did not understand him. We cannot tame Jesus or get used to him, and that is reassuring, because it means that we haven't learned all there is to learn, so we must keep returning to Jesus. A further aspect of this strangeness is that what happened to Jesus is deeply shocking, and we cannot fully get our minds around it.

When Jesus goes to Jerusalem, he knows he is heading for his death. He is given a sombre warning that Pilate is murdering Galileans, and he is himself a Galilean. He tells his audience not to assume that terrible deaths are linked to terrible offences. Here is the passage:

> At that very time there were some present who told him about the Galileans whose blood Pilate had mingled with their sacrifices. He asked them, 'Do you think that because these Galileans suffered in this way they were worse sinners than all other Galileans? No, I tell you; but unless you repent, you will all perish as they did. Or those eighteen who were killed when the tower of Siloam fell on them – do you think that they were worse offenders than all the others living in Jerusalem? No, I tell you; but unless you repent, you will all perish just as they did.' (Luke 13.1–5)

Jesus is aware that his death will appear very much like a punishment for sin. He challenges people to change their thinking – his crucifixion is not what it seems. Our thoughts are not God's thoughts.

In a book that he wrote for Lent (*The Matthew Passion*), the New Testament scholar John Fenton takes the gap between our thoughts and God's and relates it specifically to Jesus' death. He says that crucifixion was not expected, and was not acceptable. So when Jesus first spoke of his death, Peter was appalled and insisted, 'this won't happen to you' – and Jesus reprimanded him. The whole idea of a crucified Messiah was an abomination to the Jews and folly to the Gentiles. We may think that it is no longer shocking, having had centuries to get used to it. But we don't actually get used to it. We can still be appalled, especially by modern portrayals of Christ on the cross recognizable as a person of our own times, a victim of torture or genocide, killed by people who look like us. And then it also appals us when we are brought to realize, one way or another, that we have to go along the same path, for Jesus said: 'Whoever does not carry the cross and follow me cannot be my disciple' (Luke 14.27). It goes against the grain that God can lead us into pain, loss, abandonment and death. But then, if we become disillusioned and despondent, God takes us against the grain again. Resurrection is just as unexpected as crucifixion. God's thoughts are always higher than ours. So John Fenton ends with a Lenten prayer:

> Crucifixion and resurrection are more than we can cope with,
> Forgive us our resistance.
> Make us think your thoughts, not ours. Amen.

———— ◆ ————

For reflection

1 Does it make you feel anxious or comforted when you cannot make sense of God's plans?
2 Have you ever felt troubled to the limits of what you can endure? What happened? Did anything help?
3 Have you experienced desperate situations being turned around in unforeseen ways? If so, where was God in the turn-around, and where was God when things seemed desperate?
4 Are there concrete ways in which God's invitation to buy and eat without money can give us hope?
5 What do you think Jesus meant when he said that whoever does not carry the cross and follow him, cannot be his disciple? Do you carry the cross? Can you carry it while also expecting resurrection?

14

On trial – a time to speak and a time to keep silent

Acts 26.1, 9–32

What do we think when we hear Paul's defence of himself before Festus and King Agrippa? Do we smart with embarrassment that when he is brought before powerful people he gives his personal testimony and attempts to convert them?

Historians who study this period think it quite likely that Paul was put to death in Rome because he tried to convert the Emperor Nero when he stood on trial before him. Paul would not be silenced. He preached his message whenever he got the chance. He preached to Herod Agrippa II, the client king of northern and eastern Palestine, and to Festus, who was governor of the Roman province of Judaea, when he was brought before them for a hearing. They found him harmless but were not won over by his message. Festus tells Paul, 'You are out of your mind. Too much learning is driving you insane!' Agrippa is astonished that with such a short amount of time to play with, Paul should be trying to persuade him to become a Christian.

Was Paul an early church Bible-basher? Is there any similarity between his zealous witness and the street-preaching or stadium-filling evangelists of today? In the famous dream sequence of the Nikos Kazantzakis novel (and Martin Scorsese film) *The Last Temptation of Christ*, Jesus is dying on the cross and imagining what his life might have been like had he carried on living. As part of his dream he encounters Paul preaching about him, and is alarmed at Paul's zeal and sense of certainty.

It is interesting to consider the different reactions of Paul and Jesus when they were brought to trial. Both had the opportunity to defend themselves before powers that seemed willing to release them, but neither of them did so. Paul launched in with an incredible conversion story, while Jesus remained notoriously enigmatic.

I recently took part in a biblical role-play with some biblical scholars, to see what we could learn from the scriptures by acting out some of the scenes. The point was to see if entering into the stories told in scripture, and playing the parts of some of the characters, would give us insights not yielded by usual scholarly means of inter-pretation. One of the scenes we chose to play was the encounter between Pilate and Jesus. Something very interesting emerged: that Jesus was in a highly political situation, and yet he didn't pay it much attention. He spoke beyond the situation in ways that seemed slightly unhinged. Pilate came across as completely bewildered. He could not understand why the Jews had brought him this man. He kept asking, 'Why don't you deal with him? Take him away and judge him by your own law.' The Jewish official huffed and puffed, and became increasingly impatient, saying, 'We have been through this time and again, we do not have the power to put anyone to death.' Pilate, flustered and tired, having been dragged from his bed in the middle of the night, continually tried to get some sense out of Jesus. But Jesus just gave the most bizarre responses. 'Are you the King of the Jews?', 'You say so . . .', 'My kingdom is not of this world . . .' The person role-playing Jesus was visibly drained and oppressed. Pilate tried to help him: 'Don't you know that I have the authority to have you punished or released?' but Jesus did nothing to help himself. In the middle of this highly charged situation, Jesus, a vul-nerable prisoner who ought to be pleading his innocence, who could even have played his accusers off against the Roman governor, said, 'I came into the world to testify to truth. Everyone who belongs to the truth listens to my voice.' What was that supposed to mean? Pilate asked, 'What is truth?', but Jesus gave him no answer.

Paul had so much to say at his trial hearings. Jesus was so reluc-tant to speak. When Jesus was an itinerant preacher, he spoke simply but rarely plainly. His parables were simple stories but he withheld their full meaning, knowing that only those who had the ears to hear could even begin to understand what he was saying. Often he kept a mysterious silence, and gave little of himself away. Paul, by contrast, would give long explanations, and was bursting to tell his story. Had he tried to keep quiet, the words would have burst out of him anyhow.

———— •◆• ————

Personal story-telling has long been a part of Christian witness, and a part of popular, oral culture, common to human beings everywhere. Story-telling is one of the most fundamental things we do – it is how we come to understand ourselves, our relationships with others, and the paths we are going down in life. When we catch up with old friends, for example, we don't just give them the bare facts: 'I worked here, then I moved there, I'm no longer friends with Sam but I see a lot of Jo, and now I've decided to do something completely different with my life.' We tell a fuller story; one that helps to explain our circumstances, our relationships and our decisions. We want to 'put people in the picture'. Telling our story is like painting a picture: it is our main way of comprehending ourselves and presenting ourselves to others.

It can also be more than that. Paul told his story not just so that Festus and Agrippa would understand him, but so that he might persuade them to want what he has found. Paul was not only presenting himself: he was presenting Christ. In the Book of Acts, the early Christians call their discovery about Jesus 'the Way': it is a path to go down. The Apostles in the Book of Acts tell their own stories about being on that path, in the hope that others will follow. The results are tremendous. Sometimes hundreds of people in one go are converted. Within a short space of time – a fraction of the time it was taking to build the Temple in Jerusalem – churches are founded across Asia Minor and into Europe as far as Rome.

All the more striking then, if personal stories are so fundamental to us, and if they can be so effective in drawing people, that Jesus did not tell any. He told lots of stories, but not about himself, at least none that have been handed down to us. One might expect him to have worked out his sense of identity and talked about it, for example, by telling people how he knew that the Temple was his Father's house, or why he left his family, or what he experienced at his baptism. But so far as we know, it is other people in the New Testament who tell stories about Jesus, not Jesus himself.

Yet, Jesus got it across to people that he was the Way, that if you are looking for the Truth, you are not going to find it unless you look at Jesus. This, I think, was a realization that Pilate half came to in the drama of Jesus' trial. 'What is truth?' he asked. His question might have been sarcastic, or it might have been earnest, but it was being rendered more profound than he had anticipated by the strange man standing before him. His encounter with Jesus disturbed him; it opened up questions that, before he had seen Jesus, he probably thought had not needed asking.

Paul, I imagine, was rather exhausting company – someone you might want to hold at arm's length, however much you admired or liked him. But then all of us are people whom it is sometimes difficult to have around. Paul's witness involved a thought-out response to his dramatic vision of the risen Lord, while the person of Christ standing before Paul, standing before Pilate, standing before us, does not say much. There is a time for speaking and a time for keeping silent. To keep silent when words are needed can lead to confusion or indifference, or can simply mean an opportunity missed. Silence is for when words fail, when words cannot match up to the truth because the truth is more than anything we can get out minds around. Silence lets us remain where words might drive us away.

———•◆•———

For reflection

1 How would you tell your story?
2 Paul took the Gospel to much of the known world. Should we all try to be like him?
3 Can you remember hearing or reading a true life story that made a real difference to your own life?
4 When Pilate asked Jesus, 'What is truth?', he did not receive an answer. Was this because he did not wait for one, or because Jesus had reason to keep silent?
5 How do you feel about Pilate's unanswered question?

15

A Jesus we can believe in

Luke 4.14–21

What is the difference between believing in God, and believing in Jesus Christ? Lots of people believe in God, according to current surveys, including around 70 per cent of people in Britain. I don't know how many believe in Jesus Christ, because few surveys ask that question, though I wonder why not. Believing in Jesus is no small matter.

If you believe in God, you probably believe in someone or something that is beyond the universe, and independent of it. You may also believe that God can influence what goes on in the universe, so it is worth praying about your concerns in case God is able to help. You perhaps also think of God as underlying the universe as the ground of all existence, in a way that is hard to express. When we try to speak about God we find that God is indefinable. But to believe in Jesus Christ is to believe in a person you could touch, see, hear, who ate and drank, laughed and cried, and had family, friends and enemies. Believing in Jesus Christ means believing that God has been physically present on earth, and is revealed more fully in the person of Jesus than in any other way.

But why should God want to get physical? For a long time I found it very hard to see how Jesus fitted into things. I could, so I thought, make sense of a God who creates us, and of the Holy Spirit who breathes through us and draws us to God, stirring our hearts, pricking our consciences, and brooding over us. The Spirit, if you like, makes God spiritually tangible (if that is not a contradiction in terms). As I understood matters, it was by the Spirit that we experienced God now that Jesus is no longer walking around on earth.

However, that was a wrong take on Jesus, as though he had visited earth for 33 years and then left the Spirit as a less physical presence. It fails to see that Jesus is still among us. God is not just the nebulous ground of our being, and spiritual life-force. God has hands and feet, and vocal cords, and a body that can be cherished or abused. Jesus of Nazareth had all those things, and the body of Christ still on earth has all those things. 'Now you are the body of Christ and individually members of it', Paul wrote to the Corinthians. 'If one member suffers, all suffer together with it; if one member is honoured, all rejoice together with it' (1 Corinthians 12.26, 27).

So to believe in Jesus Christ affects what we believe about God: that God became human, embraced our physical existence, identified with us, and even has a partiality for the weaker among us. And because God became human, humanity is touched by the divine. The Eastern Church talks about our becoming divine. The Church in the West talks more about Christ uniting us with God. We have various ways of trying to explain just what Jesus has done to bring us and God together. None of our explanations can be totally right (because our understanding is never complete), but most of them contain helpful insights.

One view is that Jesus showed us how to live in a way that brings us to God. While that must be so, it does not say enough, especially about the changes God can bring in us and our lives when we are not even trying. Another view is that Christ was punished for our sins in place of us, making us clean enough to come before God. This image is one of the most recent that Christians have developed, and it is very popular. It comes from the sixteenth-century Calvinist Reformation, and reflects the workings of criminal law at that time: the predominance of capital punishment, and the view that punishment is almost entirely for the sake of retribution. There is one aspect of this image that I accept, but before I say what that is, there are two things I do not accept.

First, it is hard to see why punishment would bring two parties together. Consider the terrible case of the toddler James Bulger, who was murdered by young boys in 1993. When the killers reached the age of 18 and were released from prison, James' parents were appalled and dismayed. His mother Denise Fergus talked as though a further seven years' punishment for the boys might reconcile her to them, but it is hard to imagine why it would. When asked if she hoped someone would kill those two boys, she said she could not answer that question on television. She requested to meet the boys, but was not granted permission. One gets the sense that if anything were to bring reconciliation, it would be such a meeting, well handled, rather than extra time in prison. Probably no length of imprisonment would have sufficed to reconcile the two killers to James' parents and family. (The punishment anyway served various purposes, not only justice for the victims, but safety for society and regeneration for the boys.) Whether or not James' parents are able to forgive the boys is not likely to depend on the amount of punishment the boys receive.

It is especially hard to see why punishment should bring two parties together if the person punished is not the offender. This is the second thing I do not accept in the punishment model of Christ: it creates an innocent, third-party victim. Jesus was indeed a victim of human betrayal and political injustice. He was a scapegoat of the fearful, politically fraught society of first-century Jerusalem. But the punishment model makes him a victim of God's vengeance too, as though God, like us, wants innocent blood. As I have suggested, this opinion of God is very widespread. Dorothy L. Sayers captured it in the 1940s in a mock catechism that she wrote to reflect what ordinary people thought about God. On the Atonement (the question of how Jesus has made us 'at one' with God) she wrote: 'God wanted to damn everybody, but his vindictive sadism was sated by the crucifixion of his own Son, who was quite innocent, and therefore a particularly attractive victim.' Many people still think that God is like this.

It is this view of God that leads powerful people to assume they can dish out punishment on God's behalf, on domestic, national and global scales. It is also this way of thinking that encourages their stricken subjects to succumb to their blows. Evangelical feminists have pointed out that after alcohol and drugs, strict religiosity is the third most common cause of abuse in homes. This is due to an attitude that can develop in husbands, parents or guardians, that they perform their godly duty when they play the role of God in bringing discipline and order into their home. Those dishing out the discipline justify their actions by quoting such biblical verses as 'He who spares the rod hates his son, but he who loves him takes care to chastise him' (Proverbs 13.24). So while they are hitting their children they explain that they are doing so because they love them and are correcting them for their own good. And they believe that this is how God loves us; that God rebukes those he loves.

Meanwhile, the ones they punish develop an unhealthy form of obedience, based on a view that Jesus was a subservient kind of a martyr. Anita Bryant, a Christian singer from the 1960s to the 1980s, has described how she would practise 'yielding to Jesus' so as to learn 'to submit, as the Bible instructs me, to the loving leadership of my husband'. She felt that only 'the power of Christ [could] enable a woman like me to become submissive in the Lord'. Martyrs of this kind usually dislike themselves and, whether or not they ever express it, dislike the people who control them. She eventually filed for divorce in 1980, after enduring an unhappy marriage in which she struggled with herself and with God to accept her husband's way of thinking. She was consequently without work and disowned by the church that had made thousands of dollars from her name. 'Some pastors', she came to say, 'are so hard-nosed about submission and insensitive to their wives' needs that they don't recognize the frustration – even hatred – within their own households.' What would Jesus have thought of his Father, if God really were the 'vindictive sadist' that the punishment model suggests?

So I do not go along with the punishment model of atonement. Yet, there is one aspect of this model I do accept, and that is the emphasis it places on God's justice. It gives us a very strong image of a God who will not be compromised by injustice. Admittedly, it doesn't do it very well: it presents God as a bully who not only killed his Son but continues to intimidate us. To quote Dorothy Sayers again: 'He is rather like a dictator, only larger and more arbitrary.' So the God of justice gets a bad name. But try instead to imagine the God of justice as the defender of all who suffer unjustly. We would not want a God who was indifferent to injustice. The question is whether God corrects injustice by punishment. I would say that this is not God's way, and that God does not collude with our patterns of violence and retaliation.

Withholding punishment is not compromising for God. Jesus did not punish anyone and he never sought retribution. He kept the company of sinners, people who were beyond the pale so far as his society was concerned. His critics thought that this compromised him, but he insisted that it did not. He brought people to the point of forgiveness by showing them God's love. Not that he was sentimental or wet. He resisted the ways we have of holding one another down, or making one another suffer. He became angry when lesser reactions would have been too mild, and sometimes he rebuked people. He stood in defiance of the forces that mar our lives and lead us towards death. This is how he brings us close to God.

———— •◆• ————

Jesus was a prophetic Messiah, and prophets have an acute sense of justice. He identified with the prophecy from Isaiah that he read out in the synagogue. He came to bring good news to the poor, sight to the blind, liberation to captives, and freedom to the oppressed. Prophets proclaim the need for change, so they are threatening and carry the burden not only of trying to right wrongs, but of other people's opposition to their efforts. They wear on their bodies the scars for what they are trying to achieve. We've seen this in the past century in such people as Mahatma Gandhi, Martin Luther King, and Phoolan Devi. It is the plight of prisoners of conscience, and of people wherever they are who are struck and beaten for their courage, many of whom remain invisible to the world at large.

Jesus bore in his own person the divisions he aroused. He was declaring the most despised people to be children of God, and the world could not tolerate his behaviour. But his love, which burned with a sense of justice, was so strong that not even death could destroy him. Although this sounds far-fetched, and we cannot yet see how it looks beyond the grave, we can see something of how it looks on this side. I'll try to explain by some words from Barbara Kingsolver's best-selling novel, *The Poisonwood Bible*.

This book tells the story of an American missionary family in the Congo. The husband is one who tries to appease an unforgiving God, and frequently punishes his family and village in God's name. The mother, Orleanna, was at first quite blindly obedient to him. But when she meets another missionary who clearly loves the Congolese people, and who is kind to her and her daughters, the blinds begin to lift from her eyes. She can begin to see another way, and becomes increasingly aware of what is wrong in the treatment her husband deals out to her and her daughters, and the villagers in their care. Eventually she finds the strength to take action. Back in Atlanta, one daughter describes Orleanna marching for the civil rights movement: 'She is very good at it and impervious to danger. She . . . walked nearly a mile through tear gas . . . Her eyes were not even red. I think bullets would pass through her' (p. 499).

Orleanna had gone through a purging in Africa, had gained a clarity of vision and lost the fear of death: nothing would stand in her way. Christ went through temptations in the wilderness. He came out utterly uncompromised, so that not even death could stop him.

This image of Christ as protester is different from the more vulnerable images that have dominated in the past century of world wars and genocide, such as the statue of Christ as a prisoner of war that stood in Trafalgar Square in the millennium year; or the way that Holocaust theologians have likened Christ to a boy hanging on the gallows in a concentration camp. What I'm suggesting does not contradict those images, but it adds something important by taking us beyond our powerlessness and giving us the strength to overcome. If you are in circumstances that may well crucify you – circumstances of war or political terror, institutional injustice, or domestic violence – you need to know what sort of a role model Christ is.

By dying on the cross, Christ was not saying, 'Martyr yourself to those in authority, and your reward will be in heaven.' He was saying something in accord with the great prophets before him, about loving justice and defending mercy. He was calling us to stand in alliance with him against the evils that enslave us. Recognizing that this path can lead to death, he was assuring us that death will not destroy us. The difference between those two stances is the difference between the old Orleanna and the new. The old Orleanna was servile, which enabled her husband to carry on abusing her and her daughters, and the community they had gone to save. The new Orleanna fought injustice where she saw it, and while physical powers could have struck her down, as they did Jesus, she acquired a love as strong as death, a passion fierce as the grave (Song of Songs 8.6).

Believe in Jesus not because he took some punishment on our behalf, for that would leave us very passive, and still rather wretched – like the old Orleanna. Believe in him because by his uncompromising justice and love he stood against the forces of death and defeated them, so that in the end there is nothing that can separate us from God.

For reflection

1   Are you ever frightened by the thought of God's judgement? If so, what is it that disturbs you?
2   How is Jesus a role model for us?
3   What injustices are we being called to fight?
4   Should we be martyrs for some causes and not for others? If so, how should we distinguish?
5   Would it compromise God to withhold punishment? Would it compromise God to make Jesus carry our punishment?

16

Slaves

1 Peter 2.16 to end

The instructions to slaves in the first letter of Peter are difficult for us because we know that in our Christian past they have been used to condone slavery. The letter relates the suffering of slaves to Jesus' own suffering: 'When he was abused, he did not return abuse; when he suffered, he did not threaten.' Jesus could have returned abuse and threats, but he held back and managed his suffering without retaliation.

But then Jesus was himself free. Admittedly, some of the slaves in the Roman Empire had a certain degree of autonomy, since many worked alongside free men and women, and some even earned wages. But what of those slaves who were too depleted, or too fearful, even to think of retaliating? Where was their virtue? Where is their virtue, for slavery has not gone away but is rife in many parts of the world?

Today there are Bangladeshi children being stolen from their parents and taken to be camel jockeys in the United Arab Emirates. Some of them are only toddlers when they are taken. They are kept close to starvation, given no education, and when they grow too heavy to be of use they are cast out, with no money and nowhere to go. What sense would it make to tell such children and young adults not to return abuse? Many of them do not even know who they are. They have no selves to restrain.

In what way is Jesus an example for the powerless, given that he did have power? He had relative social power, and seemingly also some power from on high. And how is his suffering an example to others if it was freely chosen and actively embraced? What sort of parallels are needed for one person to know the suffering of another, and for that other to feel comfort and draw strength? Is the suffering of a free man sufficient for a slave? Is the suffering of a grown man sufficient for a little boy? Is the suffering of a God-man sufficient for mere mortals?

The satirical novelist and poet Kingsley Amis puts a similar set of questions to Jesus in a poem entitled 'New Approach Needed':

> Should you revisit us,
> Stay a little longer,
> And get to know the place.
> Experience hunger,
> Madness, disease and war.
> You heard about them, true,
> The last time you came here;
> It's different having them.
> And what about a go
> At love, marriage, children?
> All good, but bringing some
> Risk of remorse and pain
> And fear of an odd sort:
> A sort one should, again,
> Feel, not just hear about,
> To be qualified as
> A human-race expert.
> On local life, we trust
> The resident witness,
> Not the royal tourist.
>
> People have suffered worse
> And more durable wrongs
> Than you did on that cross
> (I know – you won't get me
> up on one of those things),
> Without sure prospect of
> Ascending good as new
> On the third day, without
> 'I die, but man shall live'
> As a nice cheering thought.
> So, next time, come off it,

And get some service in,
Jack, long before you start
Laying down the old law:
If you still want to then.
Tell your dad that from me.

———— ◆ ————

Are Amis' words profound or profane? They express a feeling of alienation from Jesus, as though his experience has little to say to us. And yet, if Jesus was a real human being, he had to have a real human life, lived from beginning to end with its own particular responsibilities and trials. A being which experienced every brand of suffering or every path through life would live at best some strange virtual reality. A virtual being would not be one of us. Jesus, the carpenter's son from Nazareth, was a real human being who lived a particular life and died a particular death.

Does it matter that Jesus, while one of an oppressed people, was more free than many? Does it matter that he died an adult rather than a child, that he was male rather than female; acceptable rather than outcast; leader rather than disciple? Does it matter that while he died a terrible death ('You wouldn't get me up on one of those things'), it may not have been the most terrible suffered by our kind? Or that his suffering does not encompass every kind of pain that people undergo? If we really thought this way we would have to conclude that people who have been crucified are privileged by having Jesus identify most closely with their specific experience.

Jesus did not come only to reconcile the crucified. The point is not that Jesus shared specifically each of our sufferings rather than his own, but that he knew suffering and he knew death, and in his dying he experienced total abandonment and desolation. This is how he shows us where God is. God is in the struggle against these forces of death. We understand that God was on Jesus' side because of what happened three days later, but to this day we find it difficult to say where God was at that time. Amis suggests that Jesus died knowing that he would ascend 'good as new'. But Jesus died without the support he had expected from God. Amis overlooks this. Jesus seemed most anguished not when his chosen companions betrayed and forsook him and the crowds jeered for his death, nor when he was flogged and nailed to the pieces of wood, but when he was dying and even God abandoned him. It was this total alienation, rather than the sorts of particular troubles Amis focuses on, that caused him the greatest difficulty.

But even at the most bitter point when Jesus was cut off from God, God was on Jesus' side. We understand this better than we think, because as we look for Christ in one another we know that this also means looking for Christ in the trenches and concentration camps, in the starving child, the refugee, the prisoner, and the slave.

———— •◆• ————

For reflection

1   Have you ever felt that Jesus' experience was so different from yours that he cannot really help you?
2   Have you found strength or comfort from Jesus in facing a particular situation?
3   Does Jesus' experience enable him to take on himself everyone's pain, of whatever kind? Is that important?
4   How do you think Jesus might answer Kingsley Amis?
5   In whom do you see Christ?

17

Meditations on the seven last words from the cross

These meditations are presented differently from the reflections in the rest of the book. They have been prepared with a Holy Week or specifically Good Friday setting in mind, and the invitation is to quiet reflection. The meditations are not followed by questions but by prayers. You may like to spend a period of silence after each section, and then end in prayer.

St Augustine said that the cross was Christ's greatest *cathedra*, meaning the greatest chair from which he taught. He said this as though Jesus' dying words were like a sermon, and he believed that we learn more from the sermon on the cross than we do from the sermon on the Mount. Jesus spoke seven times from the cross. The seven words are not found in any one gospel but range across all four. Several of these words are prayers, including Jesus' prayer for his persecutors in Luke 23 (verse 34). The tense in the text at this point is imperfect, 'Jesus was saying, "Father forgive them . . . "', as though Jesus were praying repeatedly for their forgiveness. It is quite possible, and perhaps quite likely, that Jesus prayed continuously while on the cross. This is something that people do in frightening and extreme situations, and something we might expect Jesus to have done since he seems to have spent much of his life-time alone in prayer.

The following meditations take the seven last words in a traditional order, as first seen in some medieval German sermons. Devotional use of the words seems to date from that time. (For this and for a number of points on the seven words, I am grateful to Richard C. Antall's *Witnesses to Calvary*. I have also made use of John Fenton's Lent book, *The Matthew Passion*. Details of both are given in the References.) Within this order, the first three words all look towards others, while the last four turn to Jesus' own self and to the work he is completing on the cross. The first three words concern those who surround the cross, and who, in their diversity, represent the full panoply of humanity. The first word, the prayer for forgiveness, is for those who are killing Jesus and who scoff as he suffers. The second is spoken to one who is dying with him, and the third to his loved ones who are grief-stricken by his plight. These words address the mockers, the penitent and the mourners, in short those who represent us and the different sides to our character. Had we been witnesses to Christ's dying, which of these words would we have received? We are witnesses to Christ's dying. So how do we receive these words?

1. Reading (Luke 23.13–25, 32–4)

The first word, 'Father, forgive them, for they do not know what they are doing.'

Let us accept that we are complicit in Christ's death: that it is the whole of humanity who crucified him. God's forgiveness is given freely to us. Do we want it? On one level we do, but I wonder if on a deeper level we do not, because forgiveness is a blow to our pride. It cancels out our status. If we are forgiven, we owe nothing and can claim nothing from others. Mercy is a great leveller. Jesus told a parable about an unmerciful servant who could not accept this. Having been forgiven his massive debt, he nonetheless demanded the far smaller debt owed him by a more lowly servant. Despite being shown mercy himself, he still wanted to lord it over others (Matthew 18.23–35).

Jesus' prayer stands in judgement over Christianity. Already by the time the gospels were written, Christ's followers were blaming the Jews for Jesus' death. But Jesus himself did not blame them. Nor did he blame the Romans or anyone else. He went to his death without cursing those who killed him. A difficulty with receiving forgiveness is that it humbles us, and comes with a duty to forgive others. Forgiveness is something given. It is a gift we do not earn. Therefore when we are forgiven, we cannot rate ourselves more worthy or more deserving than others.

So the next matter is whether we can follow Jesus' example and become people who forgive. Jesus forgave his enemies even as they were killing him: not when time had passed and the wounds had begun to heal, but at the point when the nails were digging in, the sinews tearing, and they were standing there before him, laughing.

Forgiveness, we might say, is admirable. But actually sometimes it outrages us. Can any and every action be forgiven? Shouldn't people be made to pay for their wrongdoing, or at least be brought to recognize their guilt? Jesus forgave those who did not know what they were doing. They were not about to confess or repent. Most of them were enjoying themselves and had no sense that they were doing anything wrong.

This is a difficulty we have, in becoming practitioners of forgiveness. It seems perverse to pray for persecutors, especially when the suffering they cause is unjust. We feel uneasy about parents who forgive the murderers of their children, and wonder if they have really got their heads screwed on. We describe people as being very forgiving, when really we mean that they let others walk all over them. But the mistake we make is to think that forgiveness implies a lack of judgement. If you truly forgive somebody, you have judged their actions as wrong. You have named the wrongs for what they are, but you are letting go of the debt. Forgiving those who make you suffer is in part a recognition that they have done you wrong.

A lot of current teaching about forgiveness stresses that if we do not forgive, we only harm ourselves – as though the best reason for forgiving others is to save ourselves from inner rage and bitterness. I am wary of this kind of teaching. If you tell those who are treated unjustly that they should forgive in order to heal themselves, you pile on to them yet another thing over which to feel guilty and inadequate. While it is true that an inability to forgive can harm us more than the people against whom we bear a grudge, this is not the most important thing about forgiveness. We are taught to forgive not so that we can address our inner resentment, but so that we can release people. An unforgiven person is bound by her past in ways that can drive her to her own destruction or to the destruction of others. Jesus forgave his persecutors not for his own therapy, but for the sake of their souls. He let them go, rather than holding them to a debt they could not pay. He asked God's mercy on them.

Jesus' death is often spoken of as a matter of divine justice: someone had to die for all the sins of humanity. Yet we learn from the cross that mercy wins over justice. By praying for our forgiveness as he dies, Jesus shows that God is not a God of vengeance.

A prayer
Lord Jesus Christ, your pardon releases and consoles us, but we struggle to imitate you. Your forgiveness of those who killed you makes us face our own lack of forgiveness towards others. Bathe us in your mercy, and help us to live in your freedom, so that your words and actions may become our own. Amen.

2. Reading (Luke 23.39–43)

The second word, 'Truly, I tell you, today you will be with me in Paradise.'

This short encounter between Jesus and the criminals is a moment of reckoning. In the last hour a person can be welcomed by Jesus or fail to be welcomed. It reminds me of the parable of the labourers in the vineyard, when those who laboured for only the last hour of the day still received the full day's wage (Matthew 20.1–16). It is unfair, but God's generosity wins out over fairness: mercy takes precedence over justice.

Mark's and Matthew's gospels call the criminals who were crucified next to Jesus 'bandits', which could mean they were thieves, or it could mean they were freedom-fighters or terrorists. Luke tells us that one of these criminals was compassionate and defended Jesus, insofar as one man on a cross can stand up for another. The compassionate criminal then asks to be remembered by Jesus. That is all he asks, but he is granted a mercy way beyond what he could have anticipated. Here, then, is an outworking of that famous verse earlier in John's gospel, 3.16, 'God so loved the world that he gave his only begotten son, that whoever believes in him shall not perish, but have everlasting life.'

Here are two generous men dying next to each other. Would we have been generous like the good criminal, who was the only person who spoke kindly to Jesus that day? Or would we have been more like the other one who, bitter in his own suffering, turns against this strange, pathetic man and jeers along with the malicious crowd?

The good criminal is the last person on earth to speak to Jesus before he dies. And he is the only one to offer words of consolation.

This further highlights Jesus' abandonment. At the point of his death, Jesus' plight is like that of a fallen man. He has fallen out of society, and his only solace now comes from a convicted criminal. He need not have sunk so low – he didn't get off to a bad start. Although he was a Galilean, looked down upon by people from Judaea, he had a good trade, and was presumably once an eligible bachelor. But he ended up in a bad way, executed with a bad lot. This was because of the company he kept. It is not that anyone was a bad influence on him, but by associating with sinners (literally those who had been cast out of the synagogue) and with people who were cast as impure, he undermined the social order and disturbed the peace. He eventually fell to their level and lower, to the point where he was the most despised and rejected of all people, dying the most shameful of deaths.

We have already seen that mercy is a great leveller. Now we see how those on the bottom of the pile can most powerfully show mercy and love to one another. People's insight, their ability to speak truth and to do right, does not accord with their position in society. At the point of Jesus' death, he and the generous-mouthed criminal dying next to him were the only ones to get it right.

The mocking criminal wanted to feel superior to someone. He was in a bad way, and he wanted someone else to be even worse off. It is the classic bully syndrome: if you are in pain and despised, take it out on somebody else and you feel that you at least have some control over your life. This is how oppression breeds oppression, violence yields violence, and hatred spawns hatred. But the compassionate criminal surrendered control. I suppose he knew he didn't have any, anyway. That is a blessed state to be in: the state of knowing that you lack control. Only then can you feel the relief of letting go, and open your eyes and your arms to the reality around you and accept it. God is able to bless us far more in that condition. This, I think, is the meaning of the first beatitude as it is given in Matthew's gospel, 'Blessed are those who are poor in spirit', which could be rendered, 'Blessed are those who know their need of God' (the New Living Translation says: 'God blesses those who realize their need for him'). The mocking criminal will no doubt have had some reckoning with God – we don't know what. But we do see the extravagant mercy shown to the criminal who at the last hour turned to Jesus.

A prayer

Lord Jesus, let your love of the good criminal capture our own hearts so that even when we know we deserve death, we also know that you are waiting to welcome us. And help us to be generous even in our suffering towards those weaker than us, as well as towards those who torment us. Amen.

3. Reading (John 19.23–7)

The third word, '"Woman, here is your son" . . . "Here is your mother."'

On the cross Jesus is made to suffer more than most of the people he encountered in his ministry. He is in a state of almost total disempowerment, unable to use his arms and legs. He is also in a state of utter dejection; more isolated and ostracized than the many people he sought out. But he continues his work of compassion: forgiving, welcoming and reaching out to the suffering. Here we see him concerned for his mother, whose status is probably extremely vulnerable. She is most likely a widow, and her son is dying a criminal's death.

We do not know much about Mary from the gospels. The few times she does appear she gets rather sharp treatment from Jesus, which can leave us feeling awkward and hurt on her behalf. There is an episode in Mark's gospel where Jesus' mother and brothers come to see him, and cannot reach him because of the crowd. When Jesus is told that they are outside wanting to see him, he apparently leaves them standing there, and denies their claim upon him: 'Who are my mother and my brothers?', he asked. And looking at those who sat around him, he said, 'Here are my mother and my brothers! Whoever does the will of God is my brother and sister and mother' (Mark 3.31–5).

In John's gospel we have not seen Mary since the wedding at Cana, the first act in Jesus' public ministry (John 2.1–11). At the wedding, Mary intervened on behalf of the hosts who had run out of wine. She told Jesus about the drink situation, but he responded in a way that seems dismissive and censorious: 'Woman, what concern is that to you and to me?', he asked. He did then rise to the occasion and turn the water in the huge storage jars into wine. But he told his mother in no uncertain terms that the hour had not yet come.

At the cross the hour has come. Jesus knows that now all things are finished; his work is accomplished. So now he addresses his mother and unites her with his followers. 'Woman,' he says, 'here is your son.'

So Mary is present at the beginning and end of Jesus' public ministry, at Cana and at the cross. In both cases she is addressed simply as 'woman', which is either an irreverent way for a son to address his mother, or it is an echo of the words in the creation story in Genesis, 'and she shall be called woman'. For centuries, the Church has regarded Mary as the new Eve, just as Christ is the new Adam, and as the mother of a redeemed humanity. At the cross Jesus places his natural mother and his beloved disciple in each other's care. Up until now he had held his natural family at arm's length, preferring the company of his new family of followers. Now he brings the two together. As the beloved disciple, who represents the Church, takes in Jesus' mother, he also comes under her wings.

When the old man Simeon saw Mary in the Temple with the infant Jesus he said to her, 'A sword will pierce your own soul.' A sword pierced Jesus' side, and it pierced Mary's soul. She was there to see the soldiers cast lots for Jesus' robe, the little he had left in this world. She saw the child whom she bathed and fed being stripped and flogged.

The French poet Alfred de Musset said, 'Nothing makes us as great as great sorrow.' This is not always true. It depends how we respond to our sorrows. Of the two criminals who died each side of Jesus only one showed a greatness of heart. Sorrow is not always ennobling. It can be depleting and embittering. It can leave people empty like fragile shells, or make them as hard as nails. Either way, they are unable to give or receive from others. How can we help our sorrow to enlarge us rather than diminish us, to open us out in compassion for the world, rather than to close us off behind walls of defence?

Henri Nouwen says, 'Remember, Mary stood under the cross. She suffered her sorrow standing.' Mary is in the most shameful situation, but she is not shamed. She is dignified. I imagine her as very strong at this point, holding her head high. Or, if she is bowed it is because of grief, not shame. Though her own flesh and blood is being horribly denigrated, she will not own the shame because she knows that neither she nor her son has done wrong. 'The temptation', Nouwen writes, 'is to complain, to be overwhelmed and find your satisfaction in the pity you evoke.' But if you hold your head up, you retain your dignity and integrity, and from there you can speak freely to others, reach out to them and receive from them.

One of the readings for Communion during Holy Week is from Isaiah 50: 'The Lord God helps me; therefore I have not been disgraced; therefore I have set my face like flint, and I know that I shall not be put to shame; he who vindicates me is near. Who will contend with me? Let us stand up together . . . It is the Lord God who helps me; who will declare me guilty?' (Isaiah 50.7–9).

When Jesus was no longer able to stand on his own two feet, when his feet were nailed to the cross, still he stood upright in his spirit. Mary, the other women, and the beloved disciple stood with him, and they help us to remain standing.

A prayer

Jesus, son of Mary, help us to follow your example, praying for all who are near and dear to us even in our own suffering. Teach us perseverance, patience, clarity and self-discipline, so that we may remain steadfast, trusting in the God who saves us. Amen.

4. Reading (Mark 15.25–34)

The fourth word, 'My God, my God, why have you forsaken me?'

If Jesus were praying continually on the cross, it should not surprise us that he also prayed the Psalms. In this fourth word, Jesus cries out loud the first line of Psalm 22 – a psalm that the gospel-writers took as deeply prophetic of his death.

In the gospels of Mark and Matthew, this is the only saying attributed to Jesus on the cross. And it is the bleakest of all the words. Mark shows Jesus surrounded by enemies: those who pass by deride him; the bandits dying next to him show him no kindness; even the women look on from a distance. No one offers any consolation. The desperation of Psalm 22 is fitting, because Jesus' enemies are so cruel. 'Do not be far from me, for trouble is near and there is no one to help', the psalmist says.

> Many bulls encircle me, strong bulls of Bashan surround me;
>> they open wide their mouths at me, like a ravening and roaring lion.

> I am poured out like water, and all my bones are out of joint; my heart
>   is like wax; it is melted within my breast;
> my mouth is dried up like a potsherd, and my tongue sticks to my jaws;
>   you lay me in the dust of death.
> For dogs are all around me; a company of evildoers encircles me. My
>   hands and feet have shrivelled;
> I can count all my bones. They stare and gloat over me;
>   they divide my clothes among themselves, and for my clothing they
>   cast lots. (Psalm 22.11–18)

These are words of desolation. That they come from a Psalm does not make them easier to bear. The Psalms do not soften our devastation; they give it voice (look, for example, at Psalms 102 and 142). The psalmist knows what it is like for everyone around to seem like an enemy, and for God to be far off.

Jesus quotes the Psalm in Aramaic, and the onlookers don't understand him. They think they hear Elijah's name, because Elias, as they would have called the prophet, sounds like Eli, the Aramaic word for God. This is why they say, 'Listen, he is calling for Elijah.' The Hebrew scriptures teach that Elijah had been taken up to heaven in a whirlwind, and it was a contemporary belief in Jesus' day that he came to the help of the sick and the dying.

So even in his last words, Jesus is misunderstood. There seemed to be failure in all he tried to do.

People could be that close to the dying Jesus, and still not understand. We, who are also witnesses and complicit in his death, do we understand? Or are we also wondering, in effect, why Elijah doesn't come down and save him? Why does God put Jesus through this?

That Jesus died on the cross challenges the shape of our faith. If our faith is that God cares for those who trust him, then the crucifixion seems like evidence that Christ is not God's Son, that Jesus was deluded, and that his followers were fools who were sorely led astray. This is how it looked to the crowd and to the religious leaders and, if we are honest, it is probably how it would have looked to us. The cross remains a stumbling-block.

And when we have to carry our own crosses, we ask the same questions all over again: why would God put me through this, does God care, is God a tyrant, is there a God at all? Every time someone suffers unjustly we ask, how can God let this happen? The psalmist is also trying to work out the problem:

My God, my God, why have you forsaken me? Why are you so far from
helping me, from the words of my groaning?

O my God, I cry by day, but you do not answer; and by night, but find
no rest.

Yet you are holy, enthroned on the praises of Israel.

In you our ancestors trusted; they trusted, and you delivered them.

To you they cried, and were saved; in you they trusted, and were not
put to shame.

But I am a worm, and not human; scorned by others, and despised by
the people.

All who see me mock at me; they make mouths at me, they shake their
heads . . . (Psalm 22.1–7)

Why doesn't God deliver me? Is that what Jesus was asking? His cry
may have been a true cry of abandonment: I have done my part, I've
been faithful even to the point of death, and God is not with me.
Unless Jesus truly felt abandoned, I'm not sure we could trust him
thoroughly, because there would always be the feeling that he was too
especially close to God to help us with what we go through.

If he did truly feel abandoned, then he had an unconditional
faith: a faith in God that won't give up, even when all the evidence
for it seems to vanish. This is the kind of faith that others mock:
Hah!, where is your God now? Are you so stupid that nothing will
shake your belief? There is a moral integrity to this kind of unconditional faith. I think of it as appealing to God's better nature, as
though saying to God, 'I don't know where you are but I've done my
part and I believe, no, I insist, that you are a God who will not let me
be put to shame.'

A prayer

How can we believe in you, God?

Where is your saving hand?

Where is your kindness and pity?

Give us honesty in prayer, and help us to remember when we
struggle that your own Son was in the shadow of despair.

Amen.

5. Reading (John 19.28–9)

The fifth word, 'I am thirsty.'

Jesus' last drink on earth was vinegar: wine gone bad. This was the last thing to touch his lips before he died . . . Jesus had already indicated at his arrest that he would 'drink the cup that the Father has given me' (John 18.11). By contrast, the drink that he leaves for us is life-giving. He is the one who asks us to consume him, to drink his blood, the wine of everlasting life. When Jesus met the Samaritan woman at the well, he said to her, 'those who drink of the water that I will give them will never be thirsty. The water that I will give will become in them a spring of water gushing up to eternal life.'

But for now, Christ thirsts, and the life-blood flows out of him. Thirst is a sign that we lack something we need. On the cross, Jesus lacked what he needed to keep him alive: water, and ultimately air, for asphyxiation is what finally kills a person hanging on a cross. His lack is part of the scandal of the cross. It is an outworking of that more fundamental scandal, that God could truly have become human and had human needs. By becoming human, Christ has shared with us that physical state where keeping alive could be a matter of having enough to drink. Jesus' thirst on the cross means that all who are in need bear his image.

And how do those watching respond? Is it with mockery or compassion? John Chrysostom, who was an eloquent preacher (his name literally means 'golden-mouthed'), and was bishop of Constantinople at the beginning of the fifth century, took it as mockery. This is how Matthew's and Mark's gospels present it. Chrysostom pointed out that most of us feel kindly towards our enemies if we see them dying, but that Jesus' enemies became even more cruel. They mocked the thirst of a dying man with sour wine.

But as John tells the story, those who raised the sponge to Jesus' mouth may have intended a small kindness. They wanted to offer him drink, and this was all they had to hand.

Whichever way we see the offering of sour wine – as a final insult or an act of compassion – our reactions to Jesus' need are our reactions to all who are needy. Are we kind or are we cruel? In another of the Johannine writings we hear that 'those who do not love a brother or sister whom they have seen, cannot love God whom they have not seen' (1 John 4.20). And in the parable of the sheep and goats in Matthew's gospel, Jesus welcomes the sheep because, he says, 'I was hungry and you gave me food, I was thirsty and you gave me something to drink' (Matthew 25.35). That one person's need was divine means that every time we meet a person's need, there is a possible encounter with God.

Jesus gives us life-giving water so that we need never thirst again. But in another sense, all who follow Jesus should thirst: for an end to injustice, an end to sorrow, and for the cessation of all corrupt and distorted ways in the world. Julian of Norwich interprets Christ's thirst on the cross as 'his longing in love for us', which 'he will have . . . until the time that the last soul which will be saved has come up into his bliss'. Jesus' thirst is his desire for our salvation and bliss, his longing for the world to be different. We cannot yet be satisfied unless we are somehow blind to the wrongs around us and within us. All those wrongs are the very things that put Jesus on the cross and continue to hold people in subjugation. With a passion that drives us like thirst, and which is just as pragmatic, we should long for the time when all things are finally brought under Christ's feet. 'Blessed are those who hunger and thirst for righteousness, for they will be filled.'

A prayer
Jesus Christ, Son of the living God, you died thirsting but give us the drink of everlasting life. Help us to thirst with you for the righting of all that is wrong in the world. Give us compassion on all who are in need, so that we might help one another to have life, and to have it abundantly. Amen.

6. Reading (John 19.30)

The sixth word, 'It is finished.'

'It is finished.' Are these words of accomplishment or defeat? It is all over, but has it ended as Jesus anticipated? If Jesus' cry of abandonment still echoes in our ears, we might see here a disillusioned Jesus. But this is not the Jesus of John's gospel. The Greek word *tetelestai*, here translated 'It is finished', could also mean 'It has been completed', or even, 'It has been perfected.' It has the sense of achieving finality, of reaching the goal. Jesus resolved to drink the cup the Father had given him. He already knew it was finished before he took the sip of sour wine. He tidied up the last of his affairs from the cross when he put his mother and beloved disciple into each other's care. Now he is saying: I've completed my task, the scriptures are fulfilled and the Father's work is done.

So, coming as they do in John's gospel, these words signify accomplishment, and without a note of irony. In Mark's gospel, where Jesus' final word is one of forsakenness, the cross is the lowest point, and Christ's glory does not show through until later. But in John's gospel, the cross itself is Jesus' glory. So when Judas went out into the night to betray him, Jesus knew where this would lead, and he turned to his disciples and said, 'Now the Son of Man has been glorified, and God has been glorified in him' (John 13.31).

If you have read through the four gospel accounts of the trials of Christ, you may have noticed how different John's Jesus is from the more passive and very silent Jesus of the synoptics. John's Jesus holds his ground. He talks back. He is just as enigmatic as in the other gospels but he is on top of the terrible events rather than at their mercy. So when Pilate says to him, 'Do you not know that I have power to release you, and power to crucify you?', Jesus answers, 'You would have no power over me unless it had been given you from above' (John 19.10, 11).

Early on in John's gospel, Jesus had told his disciples: 'And just as Moses lifted up the serpent in the wilderness, so must the Son of Man be lifted up, that whoever believes in him may have eternal life.' (John 3.14–15). And later on he said: '"And I, when I am lifted up from the earth, will draw all people to myself."' And John tells us that: 'He said this to indicate the kind of death he was to die' (John 12.32–3). His hearers didn't understand, and his disciples resisted what he told them. It would have seemed perverse to anticipate your own crucifixion and to see God's will in it. But John wants his readers to understand that when Jesus was lifted up on the cross, that was his exaltation, and the point where his work was complete.

When the cross seems like Jesus' bleak abandonment it scandalizes us. When Jesus speaks of it as his glory, it scandalizes us even more.

A prayer

Jesus, you died in the faith that you had accomplished your work. Guide all that we do, help us to be single-minded, protect us from temptation or intimidation that would weaken our resolve, and give us strength when God's will leads us into times of trial. Amen.

7. Reading (Luke 23.44–9)

The seventh word, 'Father, into your hands I commend my spirit.'

Is Jesus challenging God to be present, challenging God to receive his spirit, although God seems far off? Or is Jesus sensing and trusting in God's presence? Here he quotes from Psalm 31: 'Take me out of the net that is hidden for me, for you are my refuge. Into your hand I commit my spirit; you have redeemed me, O Lord, faithful God.'

The word translated as 'commend' or 'commit' comes from the world of commerce. It was used of business transactions, and so seems unusual in a prayer. The sense is of Jesus depositing his spirit with God because he knows it will be safe there. We could take the commercial vocabulary of Psalm 31 as a hint at resurrection, because a deposit is insured so that one can come back for it. Life is placed safely in the hands of God. Christ lost his life but would find it again.

The language of redemption, which is there in the same verse in the Psalm, is also financial (Psalm 31.5). It is the language of the market-place, and is to do with buying something back. 'Into your hand I commit my spirit; you have redeemed me, O Lord, faithful God.' On the cross, Jesus becomes our redeemer, who buys back our lives for God. But God is his backer. Jesus deposits his own life into God's hands.

Christ's death has been a model for those who have subsequently died in his name. And because he is our redeemer, he is the one with whom we place our spirit. So we hear in the Book of Acts that Stephen, the first Christian martyr, prayed as he was being stoned, 'Lord Jesus, receive my spirit.' Then, following the example of Jesus' first word from the cross, he knelt down and cried out in a loud voice, 'Lord, do not hold this sin against them' (Acts 7.59–60).

A prayer
Remember the hour, Lord Jesus, when you committed your spirit into the hands of your heavenly Father. Help us to do the same. Receive us as we place ourselves in God's hands, so that trusting in you we might be set free to proclaim your love. Amen.

These seven sayings are not Jesus' last words. He spoke again, appearing to his disciples and teaching them over a period of 40 days, before he finally departed and left them his Spirit. So, on Good Friday and Holy Saturday do we simply mark time, having lived through the catharsis of the passion, and knowing that the resurrection is coming soon?

No, we are waiting. Although we have the hindsight that Jesus rose again, we have only some sense of what we are waiting for. It will be more than we can imagine. Even we who know the resurrection wait in faith for things unknown. Hope is for what we cannot see.

18

Christ's suffering and ours

2 Corinthians 1.1–22

'If we are being afflicted, it is for your consolation and salvation', says Paul in his second letter to the church in Corinth.

Some of the letters in the New Testament can seem rather cavalier about suffering. Or perhaps they are not cavalier, but unreasonably demanding: 'Rejoice insofar as you are sharing Christ's sufferings' says the first letter of Peter, 'so that you may also be glad and shout for joy when his glory is revealed' (1 Peter 4.13); 'My brothers and sisters', says James in his letter, 'whenever you face trials of any kind, consider it nothing but joy, because you know that the testing of your faith produces endurance' (James 1.2–3).

These writers must have been acquainted with suffering because they were writing to young churches that were living under the fear of persecution and death. But they can sound insensitive to us, as though not realizing that severe suffering may leave people unable to smile and unable to find a meaning in life. In their letters, they were developing a logic about suffering for the Gospel. This involved sharing Christ's sufferings, being tested, and suffering for the sake of others. Such logic works best where people are suffering because of their faith. Most forms of illness, bereavement, family breakdown, loss and disappointment are not for the sake of one's faith. We cannot usually find a purpose for these kinds of suffering, and it can seem quite perverse to rejoice and thank God for them. Moreover, some suffering is so terrible that it leads us to question everything we had thought about God.

The problem of suffering is the central problem of the Christian faith, and indeed of all faiths. Why we suffer, and how to respond to our suffering, are key issues that most religions seek to address. Terrible suffering, we know, can overwhelm a person or an entire people, to the point where they lose their sense of meaning, let alone of joy. Elie Wiesel's experience in a Nazi concentration camp is often cited when people try to find God in suffering. 'Where is God?', a man asked when forced to watch the hanging of a young boy in the camp. Wiesel was made to witness the same execution. The boy was still alive after half an hour, 'dying in slow agony under our eyes', Wiesel writes. 'Behind me I heard the same man asking "Where is God now?" And I heard a voice within me answer him: "Where is He? Here He is – He is hanging here on this gallows . . . "' Wiesel did not mean that God is dying with us in Christ-like solidarity, which is how some Christian interpreters have appropriated his words. He meant that God is no longer involved in the world. God is dying; faith is dying. This experience, he said, 'murdered my soul and turned my dreams to dust'.

This is what horrendous suffering can do. And theories that attempt to explain evil and pain often fail to look full in the face the horrific depths to which suffering can take us – depths to which Paul gives voice when he tells the Christians in Corinth, 'We were so utterly, unbearably crushed that we despaired of life itself. Indeed, we felt that we had received the sentence of death . . .' We do not know what incidents Paul is referring to here. He did receive various death threats before his final execution in Rome, not to mention imprisonment, floggings, shipwrecks and more besides. But even though we do not know what outward pain Paul endured, we get a strong sense of his inner anguish, that he 'despaired of life itself'. It is speaking from this depth of anguish that Paul finds his suffering giving way to consolation, rather than to emptiness and despair.

The constructive question for us, I think, is not why do we suffer, but how can we come through our suffering so that it does not defeat us? Paul's answer is that we experience God's comfort, and by it we are able to comfort others (2 Corinthians 1.3–4).

The path by which people come to comfort others often begins from the hardest of all places: the place where God is silent. People in the deepest pain or grief can find that the heavens go silent on them. C. S. Lewis experienced this after his wife died. This is how he put the experience into words:

Go to [God] when your need is desperate, when all other help is vain, and what do you find? A door slammed in your face, and a sound of bolting and double bolting on the inside. After that, silence. You may as well turn away. The longer you wait, the more emphatic the silence will become. There are no lights in the windows. It might be an empty house. Was it ever inhabited? It seemed so once. And that seeming was as strong as this. What can this mean? Why is He so present a commander in our time of prosperity and so very absent a help in time of trouble?

God's absence was Elie Wiesel's experience in the death camps, when he felt that even God was dying. It was Jesus' experience on the cross, when he cried out, 'My God, my God, why have you forsaken me?' Having been to the darkest of places – the place where God is absent (or at least seems absent to us) – these people have earned a right to speak to us about anguish. We are prepared to hear them, because we know they have been through it.

> Every day I call on you, O Lord; I spread out my hands to you.
> O Lord, why do you cast me off? Why do you hide your face from me?
> (Psalm 88.9, 14)

———— •◆• ————

Why is God silent when we are most in need?

'But now you put a question to me asking, "How shall I think about God, and what is God?" And to this I can only answer you, "I do not know"' (*The Cloud of Unknowing*). We must be careful not to rush in with theories. Job's comforters did well when they sat with Job in silence for a week. They went wrong when they began to speak and tried to explain Job's suffering and God's strategy. There was no explanation or strategy, just a relationship to be maintained between God and Job.

So how can that relationship be maintained? How can we come through our suffering so that it does not defeat us? Job spoke for himself. He protested. Protest becomes part of our relationship with God. In this 'Psalm of Grief', Janet Morley protests on her friend's behalf.

> God I will curse you, for you are my enemy,
> and my heart recoils from your touch.
> Your loving kindness is a lie,
> and your dealings are without mercy;
> For I have seen the dying of my friend,
> and I have witnessed the work of your hands upon her.
> Daily you broke her body on the rack,
> you exposed her skin to be scorched,
> and into her belly you have thrust your knives.
>
> . . .
>
> How then shall I praise your compassion,
> and how can I with integrity bless my God?
> For like one who inflicts torture
> beyond what her victim can bear,
> So untenderly did you give her to death;
> and as one who can no longer wrestle for life,
> So did she find peace within your arms.

When we fall through every safety net, we eventually land in God's arms. To put it the other way around, we land in God's arms but we might first have fallen through every safety net. Those who have experienced such a fall never offer false hope or second-rate consolation. They do not tell you that 'it could be worse', or that 'time is a great healer'. They do not point out that 'at least you've got each other', because in fact we cannot always carry each other.

> [I]f you can't think of anything at all to say, just say, 'I can't think of anything to say . . .' . . . But please: Don't say it's not really so bad. Because it is. Death is awful, demonic. If you think that your task as comforter is to tell me that really, all things considered, it's not so bad, you do not sit with me in my grief but place yourself off in the distance away from me. Over there, you are of no help . . . To comfort me you have to come close. Come sit beside me on my mourning bench.

Nicholas Wolterstorff wrote these words in *Lament for a Son* after his eldest son died in a mountaineering accident. He is a well-known philosopher of religion. His wife Claire Wolterstorff is an Episcopalian priest in America. Claire told me that she is grateful for Christian friends who had warned them that the death of a child can drive a couple apart. It can do this because grieving is such an isolating experience. Our nearest and dearest are not always able to do what we think they should be doing for us. Grieving people cannot often carry each other, but it helps if someone lets them know that this is normal. It helps to free us from unrealistic expectations so that we can learn not to accuse each other when we do not meet the other's needs, and not to blame each other for responding differently to tragic events. It frees us from expecting to be able to give and receive from the other what only God can give to us.

But somewhere down the line we can become strong and helpful to others. This is usually what people mean when they say that good can come from suffering. There is a part we can play in bringing out the good, though it is a long and difficult process because it involves going in to your pain rather than withdrawing from it. I remember a pastor saying to me, several years after her son had died a cot-death, that the experience was so awful that she was determined to learn from it. She learned primarily by means of prayer. Prayer is sometimes described as the process of being reconciled to your situation as Jesus was at Gethsemane (a process that must include, as it did in Jesus' case, a natural resistance to the horror and injustice of one's circumstances). A major consolation for this pastor in the years following her baby's death was that she developed insights for consoling others. She experienced and passed on God's consolation, which is what Paul is writing about to the Corinthians. The Greek word is *paraklesis*, which can also mean comfort or encouragement.

This does not mean that God causes us to suffer in order to teach us a lesson, nor that suffering is justified if good comes from it. Rather, it means that even a terrible situation can be transformed. Death and trauma do not have the final say; they do not have an invincible grip on us. This is what it is to have hope. Hope is believing what we cannot see (cf. Hebrews 11.1). Some suffering is so severe that, were it not for hope, it would leave us unable to see that the power of good is ultimately stronger than the power of evil.

We cannot control the form that God's consolation takes. Maybe there is some wisdom in God taking us through the pain of abandonment. If so, I suspect this is to do with needing to let go entirely, so that we relinquish our own notions of how God should help us.

We cannot engineer God's comfort or determine how and when it will come. It might creep up on us. We might find it is there when we are no longer looking. We might give up, only to discover that underneath are the everlasting arms (Deuteronomy 33.27). Then we are abandoned to God's consolation. That abandonment makes us realize that the very source of consolation is God. This is what Paul was saying to the Corinthians: 'We were so utterly, unbearably crushed that we despaired of life itself. Indeed, we felt that we had received the sentence of death so that we would rely not on ourselves but on God who raises the dead. He who rescued us from so deadly a peril will continue to rescue us; on him we have set our hope that he will rescue us again.' By being thrown back on God, rather than by looking elsewhere to sources that cannot satisfy us, we can bring consolation to others.

———•◆•———

For reflection

1 When others close to you are suffering, how do you respond? Why do you respond that way?
2 What has consoled you in your suffering?
3 What suffering have we seen or experienced that has broken people's lives and left them unmended?
4 In what ways have we seen or experienced strength and insight coming out of suffering?
5 How can we come through suffering able to pass on God's consolation or encouragement?

19

Dying and rising with Christ

Galatians 3.23–9

When Jesus appeared to his disciples after his crucifixion, he came to them as someone who had died. He was therefore released from the confines of life and the resentments it can cause. This is an insight of James Alison, a British Roman Catholic theologian, in his book *Faith Beyond Resentment: Fragments Catholic and Gay*. Alison is describing the kind of freedom we are given at our baptism. Our baptism is, in Paul's language, our dying and rising with Christ. Easter is the traditional time of baptism in the Church, when we celebrate Christ rising from death and bringing us into new life. Alison calls baptism 'the rite of inclusion, par excellence'. It frees us from the constraints of our natural identities. It recognizes no social divisions or privileges of birth. Moreover, unlike circumcision it is not reserved for Jews or other specific peoples, and is not restricted to males.

John may well have been the first to practise such a radical rite. There were Jewish groups who practised regular ritual bathing, and Jews began baptizing Gentile converts at some point before or after John's ministry. But John was doing something novel, and he came to be named after it: John the baptizer. It is likely that Jesus himself was one of John's disciples. He was baptized by John, and he preached a similar message to John about the need to repent. He inherited some of John's followers, and did not embark on his full ministry until after John had been killed.

John baptized people in the River Jordan to cleanse them of their sins. He seems to have operated as a free agent, and his baptism was new in a number of ways. Most significantly, it was a once-for-all cleansing. This made it different from the daily washings that various Jewish groups practised in order to make themselves ritually pure. John was not interested in ritual purity or Temple regulations, but in repentance and good news for the poor. He stood in the line of Old Testament prophets who taught that God desires mercy, not sacrifice. He introduced baptism as a sign of repentance.

That it was a one-off event, in contrast to regular bathing, meant that people could come out to John and then return to their lives in the city, or in the towns and villages. So prostitutes, tax-collectors and sinners all came. They were not expected to join an ascetic community. They were not marked out by being dressed in white robes. Nor were they put on three years' probation, all of which happened at the nearby Qumran community. John himself identified with the poor by wearing rough clothes, and his behaviour was far from exclusive, secretive and withdrawn. He was there where everyone, and anyone, could find him.

John's baptism was a social leveller. In particular, it differed from the Jewish practice of baptizing Gentiles into Judaism, because John baptized Jews. That is to say, he did not regard his people as having special protected status. He warned them that being children of Abraham would not spare them the wrath of God's judgement. Birth does not give you any advantages. This later became part of Paul's message, as we hear in Paul's letter to the Galation church: 'There is no longer Jew or Greek, there is no longer slave or free, there is no longer male and female; for all of you are one in Christ Jesus. And if you belong to Christ, then you are Abraham's offspring, heirs according to the promise' (Galatians 3.28–9).

We have to question our own ideas of baptism if we think that it is about entry into an exclusive club, and if we accompany it with a set of rules about how to belong to the Church. Baptism comes with the responsibility to live our new life, but it should not encumber us, and it should not categorize us, other than to say we are now free of all categories because we belong to Christ.

———•◆•———

It is easy for us to forget what our baptism confers on us, especially if we were baptized as infants or children. There is a story about Michael Ramsey, who had been Archbishop of Canterbury, returning as an old man to the church in Lincolnshire where he had been baptized. He put his hands on the font and said wistfully, 'Oh font, font, font, the place where I was born.' How readily do we think of our own baptism as marking the time and place of our birth? I still most naturally think of the hospital in Leamington Spa as the place where I was born, and yet it is mere happenstance that I was born in Leamington. Baptism undercuts the particular identities bestowed on us by our natural birth, such as our nationality and status and gender, and gives us the primary identity of being children of God, heirs with Christ.

The new life that baptism gives us is not the same as starting afresh, as though our lives are completely rewritten. When we are baptized everything about us stays in place. We are not given new identity papers, and we are not transplanted to a new environment. The connections and relationships that have forged our characters stay the same for the most part, and all our old traits remain.

Moreover, we tend to cling to our old identities because they make us feel safe. We want to hold on to the ways we have developed of protecting ourselves and of stating who we are. Indeed, we often think it right to do so, in particular, to emphasize our gender, or status or ethnicity (the categories picked out by Paul) whenever we are threatened on these grounds, if only to achieve a balance in social relations. But, if we do assert ourselves as women or as members of minority groups, for example, we are responding in kind to the aggression we have received. Baptism calls us to be free of all that. I am not wanting to promote the *status quo* here, or encourage docility in the face of injustice. There are plenty of people who are only too willing to criticize self-assertiveness and gripe about 'political correctness' as a way of maintaining their own privilege. We need to go on addressing injustice, but we need to do so with freedom.

In his last appearances to his disciples, Jesus came to them as someone who had died (this is one of James Alison's insights). There was much that Jesus could have resented: his unjust death, the collusion of political and religious authorities, and his desertion by his friends. But he had died, and these things had no hold over him. This is the kind of freedom we are given at our baptism; our dying and rising with Christ. But learning to live with this freedom is a lifetime's work, or more. It involves learning to let go of familiar and reassuring patterns of action and reaction, and becoming new people in Christ. If we regard our baptism as just some event that happened in the past, we deny ourselves the chance to grow into it, and to gain the freedom that Christ has won for us.

———•◆•———

For reflection

1   Are there fears and resentments that shape your relations with others?
2   Is it sometimes important to assert your identity, for example your gender, your ethnicity or your social status? What if you are being discriminated against on any of these grounds?
3   What people can you think of who have learned to live without resentment, and who show the kind of freedom that Jesus himself had in his relations with others?
4   If you have been baptized, what does your baptism mean to you?
5   If you have not been baptized, is it something you want to consider?

20

The resurrection life

1 Corinthians 15.3–20

There was a convent in Ireland in the early 1960s that took in unmarried mothers. The mothers were mostly teenage girls, and they were known in the town as the Magdalenes. But instead of being honoured like Mary Magdalene, who was one of Jesus' most devoted followers and the first to see him risen from the tomb, they were regarded as unrepentant sinners and treated with contempt. One of the mothers who had been there has written about the convent, and her story has been made into a television drama called *Sinners*.

The drama portrays the convent as a very cruel place, in which the girls were shown no love or kindness. The nuns punished them by beating them and locking them in isolation. Their babies were taken from them against their will and given up for adoption. They looked for things to feel hopeful about, but any hope they tried to establish was taken away from them. One girl killed herself. The nuns wanted the girls to pay for what they had done in becoming pregnant, and yet how could they pay? What was the sum to pay, and what would be the currency? The girls' spirits were utterly crushed. They were forced to pray continually while they worked, but of course the convent did the opposite of inspire faith in them. They said their prayers as though they were the living dead.

It is some sort of anti-Gospel to make people pray to God but to deny them hope. It struck me that this community lived as though the resurrection had never happened. From each tragic set of circumstances that brought a girl within its walls, a new child was born, and yet the community never celebrated new life and never looked forward with hope. It kept the girls dead in their sins. It kept them perishing.

102

When Christ rose from the dead, he became free from the things that make us perish. Christ became human that we might become divine. When he took on flesh he infused the fleshly, physical world with his divine life. And when he died and rose to new life he turned the situation of this world around. He is like yeast infusing the dough, and because the yeast is alive the entire dough is transformed. The entire dough rises.

Christ is alive and creation rises with him. Jesus' resurrection is the first and fullest sign we have of the kind of change God is working in the world. His resurrection was not just resuscitation. It was not just a return from the grave, but a transformation. A body that was sown perishable has been raised imperishable. And this transformation is the ground of our hope. If we make one another perish by withholding love then we live as though Christ is not risen: as though Jesus suffered but did not overcome, as though God created the world but does not transform it. If by loving one another we bring each other hope, then we begin to live the resurrection life.

———•◆•———

Jesus was raised from the dead, so he is not now dead to the world: 'remember, I am with you always, to the end of the age' (Matthew 28.20). Christ is alive, and comes among us, and his influence is like yeast. Not like the yeast of the Pharisees and Sadducees who came asking him for signs (Matthew 16). He warned us to beware of that yeast, I suppose because it sets us on the wrong track. It misses the point because it is cynical in seeking for signs without making a commitment to believe. It does the opposite of working faith and hope in us. Even Thomas, who wanted to feel Christ's wounds with his own hands, believed without needing to touch. The moment he saw and heard what the others had seen and heard he said, 'My Lord and my God.' A barrister would see straight away that there was no hard, physical evidence, and would be compelled to ask: 'Could you be 100 per cent certain that this person you saw was Jesus of Nazareth who was crucified, dead and buried?' And the Apostles would probably say yes, but their yes would be a statement of faith, rooted in the new life they were living. Their life was now orientated around the presence of the risen Lord. The evidence that sustains faith in the resurrection is the evidence of transformation; the evidence of a situation being turned around from one of loss and fear to hope and love. And this is the kind of evidence we still have today, but we stamp it out if we resist love and pour water on hope. Why would the girls in the convent, who said their prayers but were shown no love, believe that Christ is alive?

Jesus did not want to leave us with signs. He wanted to leave us with love. He told his disciples: 'I am giving you a new commandment, that you love one another as I have loved you.' This love is the yeast that he leaves us, and is the power behind our transformation. When we recognize that Christ is among us, this changes things. It does not just affect how we see one another; it changes how we are with one another. The things we believe can transform our reality.

We can see this happen in both positive and negative ways. For example, neighbourhoods usually change for the worse when their inhabitants believe that a paedophile is being housed in the area. People become fretful, and occasionally violent. They sometimes group together to protest, or gang together to attack the house where they believe the paedophile lives. They become anxious about their children, and may well change the rules about when the children can be outside. These are all ways in which a belief can transform a neighbourhood. Shortly after eight-year-old Sarah Payne was murdered, one community was thrown into turmoil when some of its members got a paediatrician confused with a paedophile. All that was needed to create the turmoil was for the community to believe that someone dangerous was in their midst. Recognizing that Christ is in our midst can transform us in all the opposite ways to a community frightened by child abusers. It can make us open, gentle and peaceful, because at the heart of our community is a recognition that we are loved, which enables us to love one another. And if we love one another, and are open, gentle and peaceful, it would not be far-fetched to say that Christ lives among us.

It seems to me that, depending on how we live, we can either awaken or deaden faith in the resurrection. We can starve the belief that Christ lives, or we can nurture it, depending on how well we love one another.

———— •◆• ————

For reflection

1 If Christ is not risen, is our faith in vain?
2 What situations can you think of where people are denied hope or are held dead in their sins?
3 What can be done about those situations?
4 Where have you found hope in difficult times?
5 Do we live in ways that deaden or awaken faith that Jesus is alive? Are there ways we would like to change?

21

Loving and letting go

John 20.1–2, 11–18

Mary Magdalene is never called an apostle in the Bible – that was a title reserved only for men. But by the fourth century St Augustine was calling her the 'apostle to the apostles'. She was the first of Jesus' followers to meet the risen Christ and she was entrusted with the message of his resurrection to pass on to the others. By the second century, parts of the Church had come to see Mary as a leader, teacher and comforter of the disciples, although other traditions largely ignored her and even wrote her out of the accounts of apostolic activity.

The gospels tell us that she was the woman from whom Jesus drove out seven demons (Luke 8.2), and that she was present at the crucifixion, when most of Jesus' disciples had fled in fear. After Jesus had died she waited near the tomb so that she could attend to his body. Then she returned to the tomb, as though unable to tear herself away. The picture these stories paint of Mary gave rise to romantic portrayals of her as the devoted follower whom Jesus had saved from her errant ways.

The idea arose that she had been a prostitute, though there is no biblical evidence for this. In medieval and Renaissance times, her status as a leader of the apostles was swapped for that of repentant sinner. Numerous portraits depicted her as the repentant whore, the 'Venus in sackcloth'. And yet the New Testament itself tells us that she and some other women provided for Jesus and his disciples out of their own resources (Luke 8.2–3). She came from the prosperous town of Magdala on the western shore of the Sea of Galilee, and may even have been a business woman of independent means.

Nonetheless, in recent novels, plays and films, Mary is depicted as a woman almost hopelessly in love with Jesus, who has to learn from him to put her love on to a higher spiritual plane. This is how she is portrayed in the musical *Godspell* and in the pop opera *Jesus Christ Superstar* where she sings the song 'I don't know how to love him'. Then, of course, in *The Last Temptation of Christ*, Jesus is tempted to fall romantically in love with her, and to marry and have children with her, rather than giving himself up to the austere and terrible mission of dying on the cross.

There is no evidence to support a view of Mary as over-sexed and dangerous. Instead, she seems to have had a driving passion for Jesus for which she was rewarded. She could not stay away from the place where they laid Jesus' body. She kept returning, and when she finds the tomb empty she becomes inconsolable, weeping continually through her conversations with the three strange beings she encounters: the two angels and the man she mistakes for the gardener. She was in some ways like the lover in the Song of Songs, who searched the streets relentlessly and single-mindedly until she found her beloved:

> 'I will rise now and go about the city, in the streets and in the squares; I will seek him whom my soul loves.' I sought him, but found him not. The sentinels found me, as they went about in the city. 'Have you seen him whom my soul loves?' Scarcely had I passed them, when I found him whom my soul loves. I held him, and would not let him go until I brought him into my mother's house, and into the chamber of her that conceived me. (Song of Songs 3.2–4)

Mary's yearning and persistence are rewarded, for she finds her beloved. And then she appears to cling on to him, unwilling to let him go. Don't hold on to me, Jesus says, for I have not yet ascended to the Father – almost as if she were weighing him down and preventing his ascent there and then. Not that Jesus was in any hurry. He continued to appear to his disciples over a number of weeks. Most of them greeted him reservedly, keeping a respectful distance. But Mary is different. She adores Jesus unreservedly, and unselfconsciously. Can we say the same of ourselves?

———•◆•———

Some commentators of the early Church puzzled over why Jesus would not let Mary touch him, when a week or so later he was inviting Thomas to feel his wounds. They tended to suggest that, unlike Thomas, she was not worthy to touch him.

Mary Magdalene was not one to be deflected by the sensibilities of others. She has been identified, rightly or wrongly, with the woman who anointed Jesus' feet and wiped them with her hair. This woman attracted criticism for her extravagant and exuberant act, but she did not let this deter her. Whether or not this woman was indeed Mary Magdalene, they both display the same virtue of unintimidated devotion. If that disturbs us, we should nonetheless not criticize Mary for being too raw, too physical and too clingy, because she was rewarded; she was the first to meet Jesus risen from the dead. What she got wrong in the end was not her type of devotion, but her attempt to hold on to the earthly Jesus – an action that would have prevented God from being God. Jesus needed to go so that he could become more than just Jesus of Nazareth who had walked with Mary and the disciples. Jesus had to prise her away because they both had places to go; she out to the apostles, he back to God. He had to be reunited with God in glory, along with his flesh and his scars, so that we in all our humanity might be united with God. It was not Mary's love for Jesus that was wrong, but her fear that would not let him go.

————— • ◆ • —————

For reflection

1   Is it possible to love Jesus in a wrong way?
2   How do you react to Mary's passion, and her inability to tear herself away from Jesus?
3   Would you say you loved Jesus passionately? Would you like to love Jesus more passionately?
4   What do you think about Jesus telling Mary not to hold on to him?
5   Jesus said 'I am ascending to my Father and your Father, to my God and your God.' What do you think Mary and the others needed to learn from Jesus' return to God? What do we need to learn?

22

Unity and truth

John 20.19–29

In Eastertide, we hear the stories of the risen Christ appearing to his disciples. In these stories Christ is creating the Church. It is easy to think of the Church as a post-Jesus creation established by the apostles, and to be swayed by those lists you sometimes see of the most influential people in history. I have no idea who creates these lists or where they come from, but Paul is usually put higher than Jesus because Paul took Christianity into the Gentile world so that it became more than a sect of Judaism. There is also a very common and very powerful sentiment that Jesus was a simple man with a simple message that had very little to do with the power and paraphernalia of the Church.

But we should understand the Church initially in the light of Jesus gathering his disciples together, of his praying for them, and then appearing to them after his death. John's gospel presents Jesus praying not only for the disciples he knew, but also for those who would come to believe in him because of them: 'I ask not only on behalf of these, but also on behalf of those who will believe in me through their word, that they may all be one' (John 17.20–21). Jesus' preparation of his disciples, and his prayers for them, take us right back to the Church's beginnings.

Jesus prayed that his followers would be one, but from the outset their relationships were flawed by competitiveness and lack of understanding. So the Church was never perfect, and while we no doubt have various complaints about her, it would be a mistake to think that she has fallen from some once idyllic state of innocence.

The most common gripe against the Church is that she is hypocritical and keeps things covered up – especially sexual misdemeanours. An increasing amount of evidence about paedo-phile-priests is emerging, adding to people's sense that the Church hides unsavoury truths. Some cover-ups are a result of weakness and reluctance to deal with conflict, but some are the outcome of con-scious policy. A debate published in the *Church Times* reveals some of the thinking that lies behind cover-ups. An Anglican Evangelical and a Roman Catholic debated the best way to deal with marital infi-delity. The Evangelical argued that openness and truth were the most important thing: she thought the unfaithful partner should come completely clean and ask forgiveness so that the couple could start afresh. The Roman Catholic said that this would be a cruel use of truth, and advised that the unfaithful partner end the affair secretly and seek forgiveness through reformed behaviour. That way the spouse need never be hurt.

I had two reactions to the Roman Catholic advice. The first was horror that Christians could think that covering up truth was ever a good option. And I immediately thought of the way that adulterous affairs involving clergy are covered up, not to mention instances of sexual abuse within the Church.

My second reaction was more measured, and was formed while watching two television programmes. The first was *Clocking Off*, a drama based on characters working in a textiles factory in Manches-ter. In one episode, a father discovers that he is not the biological father of his two boys. He eventually confronts his wife and decides to tell his sons, but when he has gathered them together he cannot bring himself to do it. The programme treats this as a happy ending: the man resolving that he can carry on living as the father and husband he has always been to his family. The second programme was *Sex in the City*, a series about the relationships of four thirty-something New York women. The main character, Carrie, finally found a boyfriend who loved her well, and whom she loved. But she had an incurable weakness for her problematic ex-boyfriend. So when he turned up out of the blue, she found herself sleeping with him. After much agonizing, she felt she had to come clean and tell her nice boyfriend what she had done. And he left her. I found myself wishing she had not told him because in so many ways the pair were good for each other, and it seemed to do nobody any good for their relationship to end.

Yet, Carrie seemed to realize that if she had not told him, she would not really have held herself to account. Moreover, he would have been mocked by not knowing the truth. The same dynamics are there when institutions keep things hidden. In effect they mock people, or, as is equally important, people feel mocked by being kept in the dark. The issues at stake do not have to be sexual. It has been discovered that some hospitals have been keeping children's organs without permission, for use in future experiments. Parents of children who have died in these hospitals say they feel mocked when they are not told the whole truth about what has happened to their children's bodies. Concealing truth does harm, even when the intention has been to do good. It undermines trust and puts a kind of power in the hands of those who know, while taking power out of the hands of those who are kept in the dark.

Hiding the truth also makes it easier for people to get away with things or to behave unjustly. This is why it is rarely a good policy, even when the truth has been hidden for the sake of sparing people hurt, or of holding a community or a relationship together. There is a South African saying: 'Truth is good, but not all truth is good to say.' And yet the Truth and Reconciliation Commission in South Africa discovered the full extent to which those who had been the underdogs of the apartheid regime wanted the truth told, while those who had in some ways been protected by the regime wanted the truth to remain hidden. Parents whose children had died brutally under apartheid did not want to be spared the terrible details of their deaths. As one parent explained to the writer Jillian Edelstein: 'You do want every last detail. And you do not want to be trifled with. You don't want any flannel, any embroidery. You want every last detail, as it was. As it really was.'

The question is whether it is harmful to conceal truth in every instance. The father in *Clocking Off* felt mocked, as though his marriage and family life had been one long lie, and the anger he felt as a result was eroding his relationships with his wife, sons and colleagues. He then began learning to live with his new discovery and lost the need to let his sons know. Was this the happiest outcome, or would his sons feel mocked if they eventually found out their true lineage?

Churches try to get away with a lot of things, like retaining anti-homosexual teaching while knowingly (but covertly) ordaining practising gays and lesbians. This has given rise to a feeling of outrage. Some of that angry energy has been channelled by Peter

Tatchell's group which calls itself 'Outrage', and which goes around 'outing' well-known Anglican clerics so that they can no longer hide in the closet. 'Outrage' wants transparency, when really it is an end to deception that is needed. Transparency is not itself a virtue. 'Outrage' asks individuals to make their sexuality transparent, but why should anyone regard that as a reasonable request? However, it is reasonable to ask the Church to end her deception, so that instead of doing something she pretends she does not do, she can own her actions honestly. As it is, the burden for the Church's duplicity is carried by gays and lesbians in the Church, who feel compromised, and by gays and lesbians outside the Church who feel hypocritically judged. There is no virtue in some people being made to carry an unfair burden so that the Church can appear undivided.

Yet, there is a contrary opinion in the Church that unity is our first calling, because if we cannot get along with each other we cannot be an effective witness in the world. As one woman put it in a letter to the *Church Times*, after the Church of England Working Party was appointed to look into the question of women becoming bishops: 'The night before he died . . . our Lord prayed for unity among his followers (John 17). He did not say anything about "justice for women".' But what if the Church is not a just place for women? Is that a price we are prepared to pay for unity? What virtue could there be in paying that price? Or what about the problems of sexual abuse in the Church? If the Church covers up cases of abuse or offers inadequate compensation to victims, she is not a just place for her members who have been sexually abused. What price are we prepared to pay for keeping the Church together, and who is paying that price? In fact, there is no real unity where there is deceit, duplicity and injustice. Instead there is a mere semblance of unity, paid for by the Church's disaffected members and ex-members.

————•◆•————

The story of Doubting Thomas shows the disciples as able to be both together and honest. Thomas had an honest doubt which he freely expressed. Nobody threw him out, and he did not feel the need to leave. Christ accepted him, and shared his peace with him before Thomas was ready to accept that this was Christ.

This story steers a path between two quite different understandings of Church: one that emphasizes truth, and another that emphasizes unity. It shows that the two do not need to be in opposition.

The word 'church' means 'convocation', or assembly. One way of understanding Church is as the gathering of faithful believers. This model of the Church tends to emphasize truth. It is found most strongly among nonconformists, for example Baptists, for whom the primary expression of church is the local congregation that meets together. The Church of England also reflects something of this view. Article XIX of its 39 Articles says that the 'visible Church of Christ is a congregation of faithful men, in which the pure Word of God is preached, and the Sacraments . . . duly ministered'. In this way of speaking, people are bound together in the first instance by their beliefs, and they make church happen by meeting together.

In reality, the Church of England also shares something of the second view of the church, where the church is the assembly of those whom God convokes, and who are nourished with the Body of Christ, to become the Body of Christ. This definition can be found in the *Catechism of the Catholic Church* (p. 180). It fits well with stories in the gospels of the risen Christ breaking bread with his disciples. The story of Jesus' appearance on the road to Emmaus is especially significant, because in that story Jesus was recognized only when he broke bread. This story has been taken to mean that Jesus is made present to us in the sharing of the bread (Luke 24.13–32).

This second view tends to emphasize unity. On this view, we could be very bad at being church, hopeless at meeting together, terrible at getting on with one another, and ineffectual in spreading God's love, and yet still be the Church because Christ has established among us his body on earth for the sake of his continued presence in the world.

In church buildings, you can recognize the difference in these understandings of Church according to how much prominence is given to the pulpit and how much to the altar. If the pulpit is the focal point and the altar fades into oblivion, you know that the stress lies with belief and preaching. If the altar is glorious and takes centre-stage, you know you are in a place where the sacraments, the body and blood of Christ, are believed to make the Church.

These distinctions are over-general and meet exceptions at almost every turn, but they can help us to think about the strengths and weaknesses of aiming for truth or of aiming for unity.

The first model emphasizes belief and good behaviour, and tends more to valuing truth over unity. The second model aims for unity, because it grieves when the Church as the body of Christ is broken. Churches can become so rigid about correct belief and behaviour that they run check-lists to decide who is and who is not a true Christian. In these situations we come up against a cold, hard edge in the Church, where she stops being loving and becomes judgemental instead. It is far better to have a community that carries you, rather than drives you out into the darkness. Jesus showed us a God whose desire is to keep us in the sheepfold, rather than let us become separated and lost. Jesus shared his peace with Thomas while Thomas was still doubting.

But it is important also that Thomas was not hushed up as an embarrassment. There was no pretence, no aversion of the eyes. It is no good sweeping things under the carpet for the sake of holding the Church together. A veneer of unity that hides people's qualms and dissension is not real unity. Similarly, hiding the truth in order to hold a community together does not make a healthy community. There is no virtue, for example, in welcoming gays and lesbians into the church while at the same time asking them to veil their sexuality. Accepting people on the condition that they hide their true selves is in fact not to accept them. No one is really welcomed unless welcomed in honesty and truth.

It is easy to feel at times that we stay in the Church despite the institution rather than because of her. But it is more likely that we stay because we know her, warts and all, and so we know that she is big enough and diverse enough both to create and to mend problems, to exclude us as well as to carry us, to hurt as well as to heal. In the story of Doubting Thomas, Thomas expresses his doubts without storming off, the other disciples hear his doubts and do not shut him out, and Jesus addresses Thomas' doubt, but first gives him his peace.

———•◆•———

For reflection

1 Can you think of situations where the truth has been withheld? If so, have they turned out well? Has someone had to carry the cost?
2 Is the Church unjust or deceitful?
3 How can we keep our concern for truth without being judgemental?
4 What place is there for doubters like Thomas in the Church?
5 Is the Church a more effective witness when it presents a unified front, or when it airs its problems and conflicts in public?

23

Coming and going

Acts 1.1–11

I suppose it might be said that if God came down from heaven, God has got to get back up to heaven. Coming down to earth was not a one-way trip.

The story of Jesus ascending to heaven is partly a device to get him back out of the world. If Jesus physically rose from the dead, as the stories of the empty tomb seem to imply, then his body had to go somewhere. We don't believe that Jesus of Nazareth has been roaming the earth these past 2,000 years. If his resurrection was 'spiritual', as Paul seems to imply when he tells the Corinthians that Jesus appeared to him as he had appeared to the other apostles (1 Corinthians 15), it is still important that Jesus has now left the world. For even on a 'spiritual' understanding of the resurrected Jesus, Jesus was in some sense a bodily being and he was putting in fairly regular appearances. When Paul talked about the resurrection of the dead, he did not mean that flesh dies and our spirits float free, but that our physical bodies are transformed: 'What is sown is perishable, what is raised is imperishable. It is sown in dishonour, it is raised in glory. It is sown in weakness, it is raised in power. It is sown a physical body, it is raised a spiritual body. If there is a physical body, there is also a spiritual body' (1 Corinthians 15.42–4). So Jesus had what Paul called a spiritual body, but the apostles had to learn to live without him dropping by. They had to begin to live by his Spirit whom he sent in his place.

The controversial American bishop, John Spong, has said that since we no longer believe in a three-tiered universe with heaven at the top, the earth in the middle, and hell down below, we have to abandon talk of Jesus ascending to heaven. So he would probably not like the famous feet at the shrine of Walsingham in Norfolk, which stick out of the ceiling of the shrine church as though Jesus is ascending but has got stuck (or as though someone has just fallen through the roof).

But John Spong has missed the point. Even the biblical accounts of the Ascension do not make much of Jesus going upwards, and make rather more of his withdrawing or being taken out of sight by a cloud. Throughout Jewish and New Testament understanding, the cloud is a sign of God's mysterious presence. It was a cloud that came down on Mount Sinai when God met with Moses, and a cloud that came down on the mountain of the Transfiguration, when the disciples for the first time saw Jesus in his godly state. The cloud signifies God. The story of the Ascension, then, is the story of Jesus being taken back into God.

———•◆•———

It is important that Jesus returned to God for many reasons: partly so that we learn to live without him, and partly so that he can unite humanity to God. His incarnation was not a 33-year jaunt, it is an ongoing fact. Jesus did not shed his human nature when he returned to God. He took it with him, and so raised the status of all humanity. And not only us, but ultimately the whole of physical creation, for 'the creation itself will be set free from its bondage to decay' (Romans 8.21).

It is also important that Jesus leaves the world so that no one, no community, not even the Church, should try to claim total identification with him. Otherwise, we might make the mistake of thinking we have Christ, or that we can actually be Christ. Problems of over-control and abuse arise whenever an individual or a church community thinks that they really do speak with the authority of God. There has to be a critical distance that keeps us self-critical, and causes us to examine the ways in which we fall short of Christ.

At the same time, we are called to be Christ's body on earth, and this would make no sense if Christ was still on earth in the body of Jesus of Nazareth. If Jesus had not returned to God, we would not have quite the responsibility we do have to be his arms and legs and voice. As Teresa of Avila said, 'Christ has no body on earth but ours, no hands but ours, no feet but ours. Ours are the eyes to see the needs of the world. Ours are the hands with which to bless everyone now. Ours are the feet with which He is to go about doing good.'

Dave Robertson, a professional story-teller from Manchester, tells a story about a religious community that was out in the sticks and a bit down on numbers.

This community was told by a visitor that Jesus lived among them. And they wondered who it could be.

Could it be Brother Cyril, they mused, since he knows the scriptures like the palm of his hand, and lives by their every word. But it's not likely to be him because he has the personal skills of a brick.

Could it be Brother Kevin, who is a great person of prayer? But no, he smokes and swears all the time, and thinks he's one of the lads – can't imagine Jesus being like that.

Could it be Brother Matthew, who is very wise, and can sort out the sheep from the goats? But probably not, because he has very dubious taste and is into all the wrong kinds of stuff.

Perhaps it's Brother Gregory, who can call people to worship, and seems to have the gift of bringing people close to God. But then, he's a terrible gossip, and is always stirring up trouble.

So they couldn't work out who it was. But because they had heard that Christ lived among them, they began to treat one another with more attention and respect, just in case the person they were sitting next to, eating with, and working with, nursing when sick, and comforting when mourning, turned out to be him. And the community grew. And others came to make their homes in its surroundings just so they could be close by, because everyone began to say this is a place where Christ lives.

———•◆•———

For reflection

1 Jesus said he had to return to the Father. In what ways has he departed from us?
2 He also told his disciples, 'I am with you always, to the end of the age.' In what ways is he with us?
3 When do we find it easiest to see Christ in one another? What can we do when we find this difficult?
4 Are people drawn to our own communities as places where Jesus lives? What do we do well and what could we do better in the ways we relate to one another?
5 How can we live out our responsibility to be Jesus' limbs and voice on earth?

Sources and references

James Alison, *Faith Beyond Resentment: Fragments Catholic and Gay* (London: Darton, Longman and Todd, 2001).

Kingsley Amis, 'New Approach Needed', in *The Oxford Book of Twentieth-Century Verse*, chosen by Philip Larkin (Oxford: Oxford University Press, 1973).

Maya Angelou, *I Know Why the Caged Bird Sings* (London: Virago, 1984).

Fr Richard C. Antall, *Witnesses to Calvary: Reflections on the Seven Last Words of Jesus* (Huntingdon, Ind.: Our Sunday Visitor Publishing Division, 2000).

Alan Bennett, *Writing Home* (London: Faber and Faber, 1997).

Don S. Browning, *A Fundamental Practical Theology: Descriptive and Strategic Proposals* (Minneapolis, MN: Fortress Press, 1991).

The Cloud of Unknowing, translated into modern English by Clifton Wolters (Harmondsworth: Penguin, 1961).

Jim Crace, *Quarantine* (London: Viking, 1997).

Jillian Edelstein, 'The Truth Commission', in *Truth and Lies, Granta*, 66 (London: Picador, 1999).

Nancy L. Eiesland, *The Disabled God: Towards a Liberatory Theology of Disability* (Nashville: Abingdon Press, 1994).

John Fenton, *The Matthew Passion: A Lenten Journey to the Cross and Resurrection* (Oxford: The Bible Reading Fellowship, 1995).

Paul Fiddes, *Participating in God: A Pastoral Doctrine of the Trinity* (London: Darton, Longman and Todd, 2000).

Elisabeth Schüssler Fiorenza (ed.), *Searching the Scriptures: A Feminist Commentary* (London: SCM Press, 1994).

Holly Wagner Green, *Turning Fear to Hope: Help for Marriages Troubled by Abuse* (Nashville: Thomas Nelson, 1984).

Stephen M. Hawking, *A Brief History of Time: From the Big Bang to Black Holes* (London: Bantam Press, 1988).

M. Hengel, *Crucifixion* (London: Philadelphia, 1977).

Victor Hugo, *Les Misérables* (London: Penguin Books, 1982).

Grace M. Jantzen, *Becoming Divine: Towards a Feminist Philosophy of Religion* (Manchester: Manchester University Press, 1998).

Julian of Norwich, *Showings*, Classics of Western Spirituality, edited by James

Walsh and Edmund Colledge (London: SPCK; New York: Paulist Press, 1978).

Martin Luther King, *I Have a Dream: Writings and Speeches That Changed the World*, edited by James Melvin (San Francisco: HarperSanFrancisco, 1992).

Walter Kaufmann, *Existentialism, Religion and Death: Thirteen Essays* (New York: Meridian, 1976).

Barbara Kingsolver, *The Poisonwood Bible* (London: Faber and Faber, 1999).

C. S. Lewis, *A Grief Observed* (London: Faber and Faber, 1961).

Norman Mailer, *The Gospel According to the Son* (London: Little, Brown and Company, 1997).

Janet Morley, 'Psalm of Grief', in *Human Rites: Worship Resources for an Age of Change*, compiled and edited by Hannah Ward and Jennifer Wild (London: Mowbray, 1995).

Henri J. M. Nouwen, *The Way of the Heart* (London: Darton, Longman and Todd, 1981).

Henri J. M. Nouwen, *The Inner Voice of Love: A Journey Through Anguish to Freedom* (London: Darton, Longman and Todd, 1997).

Onora O'Neill, *A Question of Trust*, The BBC Reith Lectures for 2002 (Cambridge: Cambridge University Press, 2002).

Ronald Rolheiser, *Seeking Spirituality: Guidelines for a Christian Spirituality for the Twenty-First Century* (London: Hodder & Stoughton, 1998).

Jon Ronson, *Them: Adventures with Extremists* (London: Picador, 2001).

Jon Ronson, 'Men Who Think They Are God', in *Eve*, May 2001, pp. 40–44.

Sheila Rowbotham, *A Century of Women: The History of Women in Britain and the United States* (London: Viking, 1997).

Dorothy L. Sayers, *Creed or Chaos* (London: Methuen, 1947).

Jon Stallworthy (ed.), *The Poems of William Owen* (London: Chatto & Windus, 1990).

Richard Swinburne, *The Existence of God* (Oxford: Clarendon, 1979).

Gerd Theissen, *The Shadow of the Galilean* (London: SCM Press, 1987).

Claus Westermann, *Genesis 1–11: A Commentary* (London: SPCK, 1984).

Elie Wiesel, *Night,* translated by S. Rodway (Harmondsworth: Penguin Books, 1981).

Nicholas Wolterstorff, *Lament for a Son* (London: SPCK, 1997).

Elizabeth Wurtzel, *Bitch: In Praise of Difficult Women* (London: Quartet Books, 1998).